Richard Smith (b. 1931). *MM*. 1959. Oil on canvas, 36 x 36".
Courtesy of Richard L. Feigen & Co., New York.

Published on the occasion of the exhibition
Elvis + Marilyn: 2 x Immortal

The Institute of Contemporary Art, Boston, Massachusetts
November 2, 1994–January 8, 1995

Contemporary Arts Museum, Houston, Texas
February 4–March 26, 1995

Mint Museum of Art, Charlotte, North Carolina
April 15–June 30, 1995

The Cleveland Museum of Art, Ohio
August 2–September 24, 1995

New-York Historical Society, New York
October 15, 1995–January 8, 1996

The Philbrook Museum of Art, Tulsa, Oklahoma
April 13–June 3, 1996

Columbus Museum of Art, Ohio
June 22–August 19, 1996

Tennessee State Museum, Nashville, Tennessee
September 7–November 3, 1996

San Jose Museum of Art, California
November 23, 1996–January 30, 1997

Honolulu Academy of Arts, Hawaii
April–June 8, 1997

Curated by Wendy McDaris
Organized and circulated by DB&A Exhibition Management, Inc.,
Cincinnati, Ohio
Educational Program by EducArt Projects Inc.,
Davis, California

First published in 1994 in the United States of America by
Rizzoli International Publications, Inc.
300 Park Avenue South
New York, New York 10010

Library of Congress Cataloging-in-Publication Data

Elvis + Marilyn : 2 x immortal / edited by Geri DePaoli; conceptual organization, Geri DePaoli and Wendy McDaris
       p.   cm.
    Includes bibliographical references and index.
    ISBN 0-8478-1882-9 (clothbound). ISBN 0-8478-1840-3 (paperback).
      1. Presley, Elvis, 1935–1977—Portraits. 2. Monroe, Marilyn, 1926–1962—Portraits. 3. Popular culture—
United States. 4. Music and society. 5. Motion pictures—social aspects. I. DePaoli, Geri. II. McDaris, Wendy. III. Title:
Elvis and Marilyn.
ML88.P76E5 1994   94-5347
306'.0973—dc20   CIP
                               MN

Book and jacket designed by Mirko Ilić

Project director: Charles Miers
Editor: Mary Christian
Composition: Rose Scarpetis and Sam Reep

Editor, EducArt Projects, Inc.: Jonathan Daunt
Editorial Assistants: Rosemary Barrett Seidner,
Amy Sena Moore

Front cover: Andy Warhol (1928–1987). *Elvis I and II* (detail). 1964. Left panel: silkscreen on acrylic, right panel: silkscreen on aluminum, two panels, each 82½ x 82½". Collection of the Art Gallery of Ontario, Toronto: gift from the Women's Committee Fund, 1966.

Front endpapers: Jay B. Leviton (b. 1923). *Elvis Presley during Back-Stage Interview.* 1956. Photograph, 16 x 20". Collection J: Leviton-Atlanta.

Title page: Andy Warhol (1928–1987). *Single Elvis.* 1963. Synthetic polymer paint and silkscreen on canvas, 82⅜ x 42". Collection of Akron Art Museum, purchased with funds from the National Endowment for the Arts and the L. L. Batsford Estate Fund.

Back endpapers: Marilyn Monroe (1926–1962). *What the Hell, That's Life.* 1957. Brush and ink drawing, 11⅜ x 4¾". Sam Shaw Collection.

Back cover: Andy Warhol (1928–1987). *Four Marilyns.* 1967. Screenprint, 12½ x 12½". Collection of Robert Pincus-Witten and Leon Hecht, New York.

Printed and bound in Singapore

ELVIS
MARILYN:
2X
IMMORTAL

RIZZOLI
NEW YORK

Edited by Geri DePaoli   Conceptual Organization: Geri DePaoli, Wendy McDaris

Sam Shaw (b. 1912). *Hi, Sam Spade.* 1954. Photograph, 20 x 16".
Courtesy of Sam Shaw.

CONTENTS

ACKNOWLEDGMENTS

Geri DePaoli and Wendy McDaris

This book and accompanying exhibition required a cast of thousands, but a very special appreciation is extended to several individuals. First, we'll miss Robert McDaris, whose untimely passing robbed us of his constant good cheer and profoundly original insights. Jack Soden's friendship and inspiration is greatly appreciated.

It is through William Sena's generous support, gracious assistance, thoughtful counsel, and sharing of experience that both projects have been fully realized.

We wish to acknowledge especially Stacy Sims for project coordination and tour arrangements for the exhibition. Her efforts in balancing the many components essential to the project are most deeply appreciated. Dennis Barrie's initial support is also greatly appreciated.

The curator also acknowledges a deep personal indebtedness to Anne Ellegood, curatorial assistant, for her stalwart dedication to a daunting task, her extraordinary resourcefulness, and her continuous good spirits. Gratitude is also extended to Sandy Lowrance for her ceaseless creativity and devotion to the task of exhibition design and for her enduring and sustaining friendship. Special recognition is due Lantz Caldwell, whose encouragement and initial thoughts about Elvis served as the earliest inspirations for the exhibition. Our profound appreciation goes to Branka Bogdanov for her tireless efforts in the production and direction of the introductory video and her immeasurable contribution to the overall understanding of the exhibition concept.

Without the contributions and hard work of several key people this book would not have been possible. Sincere gratitude is due to Donald Kunitz and Charles Miers for sharing their wisdom and long experience both in literary and in design aspects of publishing. Jonathan Daunt's editorial skills and his endurance have allowed for an accessible text while maintaining the voice of the authors. Mary Christian's editing and coordination is gratefully and warmly acknowledged. Rose Scarpetis oversaw the complexities of the composition. For their expert research assistance and adept handling of complex issues we express our great appreciation to Amy Sena Moore and Rosemary Barrett Seidner. To each of the authors in this volume go special thanks for enriching our understanding of Elvis Presley and Marilyn Monroe and to Mirko Ilić our thanks for a finely designed book.

The lenders to the exhibition have been extraordinarily generous in affording so many people the opportunity to view this collection during an exceptionally long tour. The curator extends her deepest gratitude for their gifts of time, consideration, and special efforts on behalf of artists, and their ardent support for the theme of the exhibition. It is due in part to the lenders that the project has been infused with vitality and joy.

Among those from the museum, gallery, and university communities who gave their expert advice and time to this project are Shiona Airlie, Taro Amano, Diane Apostolos-Cappadona, Corice Canton Arman, Conrad Atkinson, Ken Barnes, Jayne H. Baum, Marie-Claude Beaud, Bill Bengston, Roger Bennett, Manuel J. Borja-Villel, Robert and Maryse Boxer, Elizabeth Broun, John Buchanan, Hugh Busby, Norman Bryson, Patty Carroll, Andrea Caratsch, Scott Catto, Kristin Chambers, Jean-Claude Christo, Eleni Cocordas, Herbert Cole, Pete Daniel, Robert Dean, Sydney Dinsmore, Thomas Erhart, Jr., Ray Farrell, Richard L. Feigen, Ronald Feldman, Marcel Fleiss, Angela Flowers, Matthew and Huei Flowers, Calvin Foster, Renee Fotouhi, Howard Fox, Peter Frank, Jessica Fredericks, Vincent Fremont, Katherine Gass, Richard Gault, Gerard Goodrow, Torrie Groening, Reb Haizlip, Vicki Harris, Nigel Harrison, Margaret Harrison, Lynda Hartigan, Tim Henbry, Antonio Homem, Marilyn Houlberg, Greg Howell, Henry Meyric Hughes, Tim Hunt, Jay James, Carroll Janis, Anthony Jones, Nancy Karlins, Frits Keers, Phyllis Kind, Christopher Knight, Melissa Lazarov, Susana Torruella Leval, Margo Leavin, Marco Livingstone, Joel Levy Logiudice, Lisa Martin, Steve Masler, Charles F. McGovern, Michael McKenzie, Christina Meyers, Aaron Miller, Wayne Miller, Adrian and Celia Mitchell, Achim Moeller, Todd Morgan, John Natsoulas, Barry Neuman, Frederick Nicholas, Tony Novoloso, John Ollman, Jennifer Ozburn, Marina Pacini, Laurence Pamer, Robert Panzer, Graham Paton, Anthony Peluso, Beth Perkins, Paul Perrot, Cydney Peyton, Robert Pincus-Witten, David Platzker, Pat Poncy, Darryl Pottorf, Shelley Ritter, Nuria Roeg, Miriam Rose, Jane Ruben, Simon Salama-Caro, Sylvia E. Schmidt, Nicholas Serota, Penelope Shackelford, Jack Shainman, Alvin Sher, Yoshiaki Shimizu, Lowery Sims, Alistair Smith, Michael Smallwood, Sandra Starr, Andrea Stephens, Betty Teller, Mimi Thompson, Margaret Thornton, Sarah Tooley, Margarita Tupitsyn, Adriaan van der Have, Kirk Varnedoe, Robin Vousden, Ricardo Viera, Douglas Walla, Carolyn Walsh, and Janet Yapp. There are countless others whose contributions to this project are also deeply appreciated.

Alfred Wertheimer (b. 1929). *The Kiss*. 1956. Photograph, 16 x 20".
Collection of Alfred Wertheimer.

They were two of the great icons of American pop culture, Elvis and Marilyn. Each radiated a powerful, almost magnetic sexual force, made far greater by the fact that they arrived in the mid-fifties, in the middle of a distinctly more culturally conservative, more Calvinist society, an America still capable of being shocked.

The myth of each became, if anything, more powerful and more enduring because of the tragic circumstances of each of their deaths. They each became part of the uniquely American cult of the hero/star who dies young, a victim, it would seem, of the very same adoring society that had turned them into cult figures. Their early deaths added to the power of their mystique, for they remained forever the gods of youth, and we were spared having to see them grow old. We never saw Marilyn as an aging beauty, fighting wrinkles and too much (or too little) weight, scrapping for bit parts in cheaply made television movies as she struggled into old age. Rather, she remains as ever on celluloid—young, flirtatious, sexual, and vulnerable. We are similarly spared from seeing Elvis—already at the time of his death, a little soft and pudgy, and long since disconnected from the cutting edge of the music that had made him famous—become in his fifties and sixties ever more indolent, his hair turning gray, going on some late-night talk show while hoping to revitalize his career, and hearing some youthful talk show host tell "E" how much his *grandmother* had loved his music. Our images instead remain as we would want them, of youth and energy and the kind of sexuality that was at once curiously innocent and compellingly audacious.

Marilyn Monroe was the great female fantasy figure of an era. The camera loved her from the start, catching not only her special, luminescent beauty and her rare sexuality, but above all, her vulnerability. These were the contradictions that drew men to her. In front of the camera she was different from thousands of other equally attractive young women. "The first day a photographer took a picture of her, she was a genius," Billy Wilder, the director who understood the nature of her talent better than anyone else, once said. Wilder added that when she was on screen, the audience never watched anyone else. It was, of course more than a matter of sheer beauty: when she was gone, Hollywood, which understands and likes imitations and sequels far better than it comprehends the original, immediately auditioned countless beautiful young women to be the next Marilyn Monroe. They all duly went before the camera and they all immediately sank. Where she had been soft, they were brittle; where she had been guileless, they were hard. To be that beautiful and that defenseless was rare. Part of it was beauty, part of it was the most exceptional of things, real talent and intelligence; and part of it was the genuine pain that came from an unbearable life. Just enough of those qualities managed to come through, and that uncommon combination of pain and beauty helped to produce the genuine art in her work.

What was special about Monroe, in the end, was her innocence and her ability to mock her own sexuality. Men made of her what they wanted in their fantasies. "The truth," she once said, "is that I've never fooled anyone. I've let men fool themselves. Men sometimes didn't want to bother to find out who I was, and what I was. Instead they would invent a character for me. I wouldn't argue with them. They were obviously loving someone I wasn't. When they found this out they would blame me for disillusioning them and fooling them." If men in the audience were at first touched by her beauty, in the end they were even more moved by her vulnerability, and each man would leave the movie theater thinking that he alone could save her. No wonder then that men and women alike are drawn to her flame as much as ever, more than thirty years after her death.

If Hollywood's camera caught and amplified the mystique of Monroe, it captured and systematically diminished that of Elvis Presley. He survives as a mythic figure not because of his career in movies, but in spite of it. His movies were of a piece bland and silly, and the directors constantly shrank him and softened his edges. It was as if he arrived in Hollywood as a rebel, and the first thing the men who ran the city did was to pull his teeth. In film he has a terribly soft sulkiness, and the result is a far weaker figure than the great movie idols whom he so desperately wanted to emulate, Brando and Dean. To remember Elvis, we need to disregard the movies and remember the posters of him in those early days, and most particularly, the music—and the earlier, the better.

To remember him, we have to recall Elvis as he was when he burst upon the American cultural scene in the mid-fifties: crude, unsophisticated, a dark comet shooting into a bland conventional pop music scene, a kind of early musical Darth Vader with his guitar and androgynous looks, the bane of ministers and parents alike. He was a country boy whom Hollywood uprooted from the country and separated from what had made him artistically special.

It was the special tragedy of his career that his agent-promoter, Colonel Tom Parker—seeking to prolong his career, underestimating the great cultural phenomenon that was taking place in front of him, sure that a country singer had a short career span—took him from what he did best, which was performing live in front of his own people (in general, the countrier and younger the audience, the better the performance), where his work had a raw, almost unconscious sexuality to it, and turned him into a listless B-movie Hollywood actor. Thus shorn of his roots and his edge, we watched his vitality and legitimacy steadily seep away, and his innate sense of self become diminished.

Elvis Presley was an American original, the rebel as mother's boy, alternately sweet and sullen, ready on demand to be either respectable or rebellious. When he finally made it big, the first thing he did was give his mother a Cadillac, even though she did not know how to drive. His music was instinctive, he was self-taught and could not read a note, and his success was visceral. It needed no promotion or huckstering. The first time a Memphis disk jockey played his records, the switchboard at the station lit up all night. It was the truest of American success stories: one day he was a virtual failure, driving a truck for $1.65 an hour (he liked driving a truck, it gave a country boy like Elvis a sense of freedom that his previous job, working in a munitions factory, had not), and the next day he was on his way to leading a revolution in music and in culture.

He grew up in places, first in North Mississippi and then in Memphis, which though nominally segregated in those days were at the confluence of great and differing strains of indigenous American music: black gospel, white country, and black blues. Those different strands were woven into his own music. His parents, poor, white, Pentecostal churchgoing people, hearing his music for the first time, thought it was sinful, though in time they, too, came around. He became, much to his own surprise, a figure of great historical importance, the first white singer to make it big by singing and incorporating the beat of black music. "Before Elvis," John Lennon, one of his lineal descendants, once said, "there was nothing."

The beat was critical. When a Memphis disk jockey who specialized in rock first played Elvis' music, he emphasized again and again over the radio that Elvis went to Humes High, which meant that every young person listening in Memphis knew that Presley was white. He had an intuitive sense of early American teenage punk (or softcore hood) long before it was fashionable, and he did it in a poor part of the country not hospitable to a style so revolutionary: the long hair pomaded both up and down, the collar of his shirt or jacket up in back, the black pegged pants, the black and pink jackets that seemed designed to be worn by a pimp. If he lacked Brando's and Dean's talent on the screen, he was nonetheless very much a part of the new American tradition of youthful self-absorption and narcissism.

Elvis' first great contribution to what became an ongoing cultural revolution was that he was the first important racial crossover figure in music, the first white to use the black beat with such success, his even more lasting contribution was that he was the leader of a larger revolution, the coming of a youth culture. After he burst upon the scene we had a new chasm in our society: it seemed to align the young on one side in almost all things—clothes, music, life-styles—and their parents on the other. Years later, the great American conductor–composer Leonard Bernstein said Elvis was "the greatest cultural force in the twentieth century." When a cerebral friend questioned Bernstein how that could be, this hillbilly guitarist who ground his hips on stage for teenagers and whined aloud about hound dogs, the composer answered, "He introduced the beat to everything, and he changed everything, music, language, clothes, it's a whole new social revolution—the sixties comes from it. Because of him, a man like me barely knows his musical grammar any more."

Willem de Kooning (b. 1904). *Marilyn Monroe.* 1954. Oil on canvas, 50 x 30".
Collection of the Neuberger Museum of Art, Purchase College, State University of New York; gift of Roy R. Neuberger.

In his great film of 1947, *Late Spring,* Yasujiro Ozu signaled the dawning of a new age by showing Coca-Cola signs in Japanese neighborhoods. Not long after the war, the spread of American pop culture had advanced to the point where it seemed that the Coke logo was probably the most recognized visual signifier in the world. Recently while traveling, I've wondered whether even that sign has not been outstripped in ubiquity by the Marlboro Man, a symbol of America as a place of adventure, independence, and rugged individualism.

But the export of American pop culture has not been entirely by advertising designs, nor has it been wholly Euro-ethnic. Sometime in the 1970s, not long after the Thrilla in Manila, I read of a study that indicated that the person with the highest recognition percentage globally—more even than, say, Nixon or Mao—was Muhammad Ali. While in China at the time Michael Jackson's *Bad* album was about to be received in the stores, I read in the papers of Chinese youth standing for literally days and nights outside the stores in the hope of getting a copy. By 1987 breakdancing was a craze, widespread from Ireland to China. Madonna, of course, is everywhere now, too.

But beneath the images of Michael and Madonna, beneath Michael's moonwalk and Madonna's *Sex* book, lie the ghostly presences of Elvis and Marilyn, perhaps the most enduring symbols of this unprecedented global cultural dominance of a composite nation with no clear cultural identity. In 1987, in writing about the reception in the United States of contemporary art from Africa, I referred to America's postwar exports as "Cocacolonialism, Elvis, Marilyn." What's it about? Why these two? Why have we all become more or less their devotees, no matter what skepticism about them we may have?

Elvis and Marilyn are both figures who have come to be known more or less globally by only one name—like Jesus, Napoleon, or Rasputin. And one of them, Elvis, belongs to the even smaller and more elite rank of those who are forever known as the inhabitants of empty tombs—again like Jesus.

It's interesting to ask what aspect of America these haunting figures represent. If the Marlboro Man is a symbol of competence and autonomy—of America as both a lone rider and a global enforcer—Elvis and Marilyn are very different. They seem primarily to represent vulnerability, perhaps because both attained their mythic status in the early to middle 1950s, just slightly before American military and geopolitical hegemony began to emerge from isolation. Both represent the innocence of America at mid-century, just at the moment of its burgeoning ascendancy, when the nation still seemed to be the America of Mickey Mantle and GI Joe, before the darknesses of its foreign and domestic policies—the McCarthy Era, the Cold War, the war in Vietnam—became overt.

In the aftermath of those sobering events and revelations, one no longer believes so simply in American innocence and vulnerability. Yet Elvis and Marilyn remain, hovering archetypally over us and over much of the rest of the world. Perhaps it is now a nostalgic yearning for that moment of innocence they represent, rather than a present celebration of it. Elvis and Marilyn, like figures from religion or mythology, are wrapped in an enigma today that they could not have foreseen in their time. The authors in this book shed the light of their own learning and sensibilities upon it.

Elvis + Marilyn: 2 x Immortal is a visual and conceptual consideration of the phenomenon of Elvis Presley and Marilyn Monroe in our time. This book is not about high, low, or popular culture, but more about the dissolution or leveling of these previously codified hierarchies. When research for this project began in 1988, we expected that the art and writing would address popular culture. In fact, we organized an academic conference entitled "Icons of Popular Culture: Elvis & Marilyn" in order to investigate the subject. However, after reviewing the proposals and looking at art depicting Elvis and Marilyn from around the world, it became clear that the evidence of our pursuit did not conform to those initial expectations. Instead, the variety of works of art and essays from various academic disciplines speak of a transformation from the physical to the spiritual and of the myth-making process. This book offers the opportunity to witness the transfiguration of Elvis and Marilyn from a cultural state of stardom to an iconic state of spiritual and religious resonance.

Just as it is said that the story of Christ may be the world's best-known story, it can be said that portraits of Elvis and Marilyn are among the world's most famous images. Since the death of Elvis Presley in 1977, his persona has been transformed from star to legend to myth to icon. Marilyn Monroe's transformation occurred several years after her death in 1962. Each passed through these stages in different ways, each marked by artists who show the first awareness and in fact facilitate the process. While we cannot pinpoint exactly the particular moment at which each transformative stage from star to icon occurs, the community of these works of art and essays indicates that something is in process.

The issue this collection of essays raises is about a proclamation of a new faith in a time—defined by some as postmodern—that is marked by the end of the grand narrative, of the fixed perspective, of marked high or low culture, and of predictable beginnings, middles, and ends. It is a time of transition. This is most apparent when we consider that although the pervasive influence of Andy Warhol's riveting images of Elvis and Marilyn from the 1960s is evident in many of the works, these artists go beyond Warhol and an overly simplistic definition of Pop art as invoking popular imagery.[1]

The works of art in this book are about Elvis and Marilyn, but they are also about a new way of seeing, one that challenges the current holdover of a nineteenth-century visual language. Although the works of art represent a variety of media, the images come to you here by way of photography. It bears remembering that a photograph pictures a segment of the world from the perspective of one eye and it freezes time. It denies the viewer participation and makes one an outside observer.

Therefore, this book is organized around the premise that words carry their ideas within the framework of verbal language while images deliver their meaning by way of visual language. One set of statistics, produced by a Getty Foundation study, places over 90 percent of the American population among the visually illiterate. It therefore is no surprise that many people depend on words to access a work of art: we encourage you also to read the images for what they communicate. The art here is interactive with the essays and operates in a way parallel to and mutually independent of them. Its visual language and conventions reveal a transition away from references to popular culture, toward myth-making and spirituality.

Roger Shimomura (b. 1939). *Heroine, Hammer, Hibachi.* 1987. Acrylic on canvas,
60 x 24". Courtesy of the artist.

I read somewhere that Napoleon said a golden statue should be erected to Thomas Paine in every city in America.
I remembered this in the late seventies when I saw Elvis in his gold lamé suit.
Conrad Atkinson

Conrad Atkinson (b. 1940). *For Thomas Paine; For Elvis Presley.* 1985.
Mixed media, 102 x 61". Courtesy of Ronald Feldman Fine Arts, New York.

As with any mythological process, the time has passed for concern about the truth or fiction of various details of the lives of Elvis and Marilyn. They have transcended the specific. We read of Elvis and Marilyn having been sacrificed for our sins in many of the artists' statements and in the ideas expressed by some visitors to Graceland at Tribute Week, the cultural event commemorating Elvis' death. The reality of their actual lives is less important than the way in which these figures are pictured. Stories told about them and scholarly analyses by specialists—from theologian to psychologist to literary critic—tell us of their images carrying and mirroring the needs and projections of a culture in the midst of upheaval and value shifts.

The contributors to this volume represent various disciplines. David Halberstam, a Pulitzer Prize–winning journalist whose many books on the cultural life during this era include the best-seller *The Fifties*, reflects on the sensation that Elvis and Marilyn each spawned during their lives and the origins of the myths perpetuated after their deaths. Thomas McEvilley, author of *Art and Otherness* and a specialist in postmodern multicultural issues, considers the power and ubiquity of images of Elvis and Marilyn in our culture. Bono of U2 expands on the diverse aspects of Elvis Presley. Richard Martin, an art historian and director of the Costume Institute at the Metropolitan Museum of Art in New York, provides an art historical analysis of a work about Marilyn Monroe by Richard Hamilton. John Baskerville applies methodology from African-American literary criticism to an analysis of the music of Elvis Presley, and in doing so, makes a vital point regarding critical value judgments and standards of measure. Kate Millett, a noted writer, poet, artist, and critic, uses her feminist perspective to deliver her personal and powerful thoughts about Marilyn in the context of society then and now. Bruce Heller, University of California, San Francisco, and Alan Elms, University of California, Davis, both professors of psychology, use the analytical methods of psychology and the relatively new device of psychobiography to give an intimate view of the personality of Elvis Presley and a proposal about the nature of his charisma. Lucinda Ebersole, an American studies and feminist scholar and editor of the recently published *Mondo Elvis*, uses an interdisciplinary approach combining cultural studies, religious studies, and literature to point to the literary evidence of the creation of icons from both the ubiquitous images and the transformed lives of Elvis and Marilyn. Gary Vikan, a Byzantinist and the director of the Walters Art Gallery in Baltimore, combines the approaches of art history, cultural anthropology, and comparative religious studies to show the uncanny parallels between the medieval pilgrimage process and the activities surrounding Graceland. Each of these essays offers the reader an opportunity to gain insight into the process of mythological transformation as well as an understanding of the tools and methods used within different disciplines of study.

What we have gathered here are the coins of a realm in which Elvis and Marilyn, multivalent icons, have been peculiarly anointed king and queen, god and goddess, in ways that exceed the sum of our admiration or apprehension, by a broadly diverse group of writers, scholars, and artists.

Carlos Pazos (b. 1949). *Tu Perro Te Recuerda*. 1989. Mixed media, 98⁷⁄₁₆ x 51³⁄₁₆ x 29 ⅝".
Courtesy of Galeria Joan Prats, Barcelona.

elvis
son of tupelo
elvis
mama's boy
elvis
the twin brother of Jesse who died at birth and
was buried in a shoe box
elvis
drove a truck
elvis
was recorded at sun studios by the musical diviner
sam phillips
elvis
was managed by colonel tom parker, an ex–carny
barker whose last act was a singing canary
elvis
was the most famous singer in the world since
king david
elvis
lived on his own street
elvis
liked to play speedcop
elvis
had a monkey named bubbles before anyone
elvis
wore a cape at the white house when he
was presenting nixon with two silver pistols
elvis
was a member of the drug squad
elvis
wore eye make up, just hangin' out
elvis
wore a gold nudie suit and trained his lip to curl
elvis
was macho, but could sing like a girl
elvis
was not a big talker
elvis
was articulate in every other way
elvis
died his hair black to look like valentino
elvis
held a microphone the way valentino held nita
naldi in blood and sand
elvis
dressed black long before he dressed in black
elvis
sang black except in lower registers
where he was a student of dean martin
elvis
admired mario lanza
elvis
delivered the world from crooning
elvis
was a great crooner
elvis
had a voice that could explain the sexuality of
america
elvis
was influenced by jim morrison in his choice of
black leather for the '68 comeback special
elvis
invented the beatles
elvis
achieved world domination from a small town
elvis
was conscious of myth
elvis
had pharaoh-like potential
elvis
was made by america, so america could remake
itself

elvis
had good manners
elvis
was a bass, a baritone, and a tenor
elvis
sang his heart out at the end
elvis
the opera
elvis
the soap opera
elvis
loved america, God, the bible, firearms, the
movies, the office of presidency, junk food, drugs,
cars, family, television, jewelry, straight talkin', dirty
talkin', game shows, uniforms, and self-help books
elvis
like america, wanted to improve himself
elvis
like america, started out loving but later turned on
himself
elvis'
body could not stop moving
elvis
is alive, we're dead
elvis
the charismatic
elvis
the ecstatic
elvis
the plastic
elvis
the elastic
with a spastic dance that might explain the energy
of america
elvis
fusion and confusion
elvis
earth rod in a southern dorm
elvis
shaking up an electrical storm
elvis
in Hollywood his voice gone to ground
elvis
in las vegas with a big brassy sound
elvis
the first rock and roll star with scotty moore, bill
black, and d. j. fontana
elvis
with james burton and ronny tutt
elvis
the movie star made three good films:
viva las vegas, flaming star, and jailhouse rock
elvis
the hillbilly brought style to passion, kitsch to an
art form and shoes center stage
elvis
the musician brought rhythm to the white race,
blues to pop, and rock and roll to
wherever rock and roll is
elvis
the pelvis, swung from africa to europe, which is
the idea of america
elvis
liberation
elvis
the kung fu would come later
elvis
hibernation
elvis
built a mansion he called Graceland, later to
become a theme park

elvis
woke up to whispers
elvis
thought of himself as a backslider
elvis
knew guilt like a twin brother
elvis
called God every morning
then left the phone off the hook
elvis
turned las vegas into church
when he sang "love me tender"
elvis
turned america into a church
when he sang "the trilogy"
elvis
was harangued by choice;
flesh vs. spirit, God vs. rock and roll
mother vs. lover, father vs. the colonel
elvis
grew sideburns as a protest against tom jones'
hairy chest
elvis
would have a president named after him
elvis
was one of the boys
elvis
was not one of the boys
elvis
had an acute intelligence disguised as talent
elvis
broke priscilla's heart
elvis
broke lisa marie's heart
elvis
woke up my heart
elvis
white trash
elvis
the memphis flash
elvis
didn't smoke hash
and woulda been a sissy
without johnny cash
elvis
didn't dodge the draft
elvis
had his own aircraft
elvis
having a laugh
on the lisa marie
in a color photograph
elvis
under the hood
elvis
cadillac blood
elvis
darling bud flowered and returned
to the mississippi mud
elvis
ain't gonna rot
elvis
in a memphis plot
elvis
didn't hear the shot
but dr. king died
just across the lot from
elvis
vanilla ice cream
elvis
girls of 14

elvis
memphis spleen
shooting at the tv
reading Corinthians 13
elvis
with God on his knees
elvis
on three tv's
elvis
here come the killer bees
head full of honey
potato chips and cheese
elvis
the bumper stickers
elvis
the white knickers
elvis
the white nigger
ate at burger king
and just kept getting bigger
elvis
sang to win
elvis
"the battle hymn"
elvis
the battle to be slim
elvis
ate america
before america ate him
elvis
stamps
elvis
necromance
elvis
fans
elvis
psychophants
elvis
the public enemy
elvis
don't mean shit to chuck d
elvis
changed the center of gravity
elvis
made it slippy
elvis
nixon
elvis
christ
elvis
Jackson
elvis
Marcus
elvis
the pelvis
elvis
the psalmist
elvis
the genius
elvis
the generous
elvis
forgive us
elvis
pray for us
elvis
aaron presley
(1935–1977)

YOU'RE RIGHT, I'M LEFT, HE'S GONE

Moiseiwitsch

Carel Moiseiwitsch (b. 1941). *You're Right, I'm Left, He's Gone.* 1993. Pastel on
paper, 30 x 22½". Collection of Bob and Lasha Roche, Vancouver.

James Rosenquist (b. 1933). *Marilyn Monroe, I.* 1962. Oil and spray enamel on canvas, 93 x 72¼". The Museum of Modern Art, New York; the Sidney and Harriet Janis Collection. © James Rosenquist/VAGA, New York 1994.

Altar to Self-Indulgence and Decadence is a rethinking of a traditional Christian altar. The central holy figure is an embracing, receptive, and seductive Marilyn Monroe as the Great Mother. The Great Mother is surrounded by the elements that elevate and debase her simultaneously. To her right, Marilyn is drawn into the shallow attractions of fashion and rock imagery. To her left, Marilyn is tempted by the corruption of monarchy and the church. The prayers of the "altar" are expressed in rock lyrics. Personal hopes, narratives, and threats are quoted from Iggy Pop, David Bowie, Robert Smith, and Debbie Harry. The sensuous and corrupt words console the penitent viewer.

Michael and Heather Martin-Daniels

Michael Martin-Daniels (b. 1963) & Heather Martin-Daniels (b. 1963). *Altar to Self-Indulgence and Decadence.* 1988. Mixed-media assemblage, 71 x 83 x 13" (opened). Courtesy of the artists.

Andy Warhol (1928–1987). *Elvis I and II*. 1964. Left panel: silkscreen on acrylic; right panel: silkscreen on aluminum, each panel, 82½ x 82½". Collection of the Art Gallery of Ontario, Toronto; gift from the Women's Committee Fund, 1966.

The title of my painting Double Elvis *is of course lifted from a painting by Andy Warhol. Somehow the idea that Elvis could be double—repeated or cloned—appealed to me. The actual structure of my painting alludes to a completely different work, however. I was thinking of Frank Stella's painting,* Jasper's Dilemma, *which is constructed of two squares placed side by side, each made up of mitered concentric bands. The square on the right is painted in shades of gray, the one on the left in spectrum colors.*
Peter Halley

Peter Halley (b. 1952). *Double Elvis.* 1990. Acrylic and Roll-a-Tex on canvas. 90½ x 190".
Collection of Cooperfund, Inc.

Richard Pettibone (b. 1938). *Andy Warhol, Elvis. 1964*. 1971. Silkscreen on canvas, 8¾ x 8¼".
Tom Patchett collection, Los Angeles; courtesy Curt Marcus Gallery, New York.

We tasted forbidden fruit in his curled lip and bedroom eyes. We danced to his multicultural beat thirty years before intellectuals gave it a name. Yeah, Elvis was a troublemaker; his waterfall and ducktail gave us back the hair Eisenhower had shaved from our fathers' heads. Elvis was a throwdown ladies' man who could take care of himself. He would rather sing than fight, but when trouble came he never backed off. For five years the rocking was good.

Jerry Kearns

Jerry Kearns (b. 1943). *Earth Angel.* 1989. Acrylic on canvas, 76 x 100".
Courtesy of the artist and Kent Gallery, New York.

In 1988 I became aware that a great many artists in the South were producing works of art with a reference to Elvis Presley. The Southeastern Center for Contemporary Art in Winston-Salem, North Carolina, had created an invitational exhibit in 1987 that featured art exclusively devoted to this subject. At the same time, Marilyn Monroe's importance seemed of equal value—I had become aware of a 1967 show in New York at the Sidney Janis Gallery entitled *Homage to Marilyn Monroe,* in which works by many of the stellar artists of the time were exhibited. Here, then, was proof that Andy Warhol's powerful depictions of Elvis and Marilyn were not isolated fascinations. It was clear to me that something was afoot.

In the early days of research, four topics prompted by the works of art about Elvis and Marilyn repeatedly came to the fore: first, their images were strongly emblematic and recognizable as part of popular culture along with sports figures, flags, product names, song titles, and advertisements. Second, their images were not only emblematic but larger than life and worthy of adulation and emulation. Third, Elvis and Marilyn appeared in contradictory form themselves in these images—they were direct and unfathomable, beloved and despised, accomplished and unrealized, knowing and naive, comic and tragic, exaggeratedly beautiful and beautifully exaggerated, overflowing with physical vitality and gravely unhealthy, refined and obtuse—all fascinating and perplexing dualities. Fourth, and on a more elevated level, the iconography and formal language some artists used in their representations of Elvis and Marilyn indicated a distinctly religious direction. These four observations, then, coupled with enthusiastic responses to my queries, compelled me to explore their further implications.

The works in this book have been produced in a dazzling variety of media by well-known and not-so-well-known artists. Spanning the years from 1955 to 1993, they form a resonant, integrated collection, and each individual work amplifies, echoes, expands, and supports the others while expressing its own unique set of visual associations. At the same time, however, the collection divides itself into groups. The first division, cultural, includes works that reflect both negative and positive aspects of culture as well as its constant state of change. Cultural commentary in these works contains evidence of the elevation of Marilyn and Elvis to heroic stature.

Within the cultural division, the works of Andy Warhol are perhaps the most recognizable and frequently quoted. *Elvis I and II* (p. 22) is an evocation of America, the American West, the frontier spirit, and Hollywood as America's lost frontier. Here, in the transitory experience of a movie, everyone can achieve his dreams.

The two identically sized panels of the work form a discourse on relationships and comparisons. What do these relationships and comparisons suggest? First, there is a juxtaposition between the vulnerable and fearful expression on Elvis' face and the position of the threatening gun. There is a suggestion that without the gun Elvis would be harmless (or that without the viewer's assumption of his masculinity, Elvis' persona easily dissembles into a feminine vulnerability). Second, one can draw a comparison between the overly dramatic colors of the left panel—expressions of fantasy or even a drag sensibility—and the laconic description in shades of black and gray on the right—an apparition, afterimage, or cultural artifact. The relative presence or absence of color may suggest a comparison between the moving image of television or film and the static powers of print media. Relative to this last comparison is a deeper level of discourse—*Elvis I and II* is a bold challenge to the viewer to address many issues: the identity of American manhood, the surfeit of the cinematic image in American culture and its implied passive human target, the American love affair with guns and violence, and the idea that Elvis as cowboy seems far more potent as an American symbol than Elvis as Elvis.

Richard Pettibone, who early on recognized Warhol's work as permission to appropriate (or borrow and quote) works of art, created *Andy Warhol, Elvis, 1964* (p. 24)—a close appropriation of Warhol's *Double Elvis.* The differences are indiscernible to the viewer who has not experienced an original Warhol work. By changing the colors of the original, Pettibone reflects the subtle and sometimes not-so-subtle changes that occur in the reproduction of works of art in twentieth-century print media. Pettibone demands that the viewer see the work he has appropriated by altering the scale of the original—almost always compulsory for reproductions of art. Is Pettibone also critiquing a culture whose appreciation of art is almost invariably secondhand? Can repetition contribute to the attainment of fame? His appropriation is apt, for Warhol's oeuvre also is pregnant with statements about appropriation in print and other media, along with the concomitant cultural implications.

Warhol's intuition about Elvis and Marilyn as consummate cultural symbols has been confirmed by multiple iterations, each with its own unique spin. Artistic repetitions, appropriations, and quotations are iconoclastic as well as reverential. By juxtaposing the quotation with overlays, artists

simultaneously pay homage to and toll the death knell for the original source. Quotation art expresses relative time's encroaching dominance over linear time.

Jerry Kearns' *Earth Angel* (p. 25) appropriates Warhol's cowboy Elvis and transforms him from merely threatening to actively murderous through overlays of key journalistic images from the late 1960s and early 1970s (a young Vietnamese girl running in pain and terror and an anguished American college student at Kent State University). These unforgettable images are in themselves icons for those who lived through the Vietnam era. Kearn's use of them underscores the artist's heightened ability to select potent images from his surroundings.

The archaeological layers of print and film media speak of cultural

layers in *Marilyn* (p. 39) by Mimmo Rotella, who lives and works in Milan. We gain access to this work through the cultural tradition of the movie poster. Layers of meaning peel off with the visual associations. At second glance, however, the rings left by the remains of previous posters form an aura around Marilyn that is vaguely reminiscent of religious iconography. But Marilyn is not the Virgin—her blond hair forms a bold crown, the immodest necklace of jewels lies upon her bare shoulders, her expression smolders with arousal. As she once beckoned to us from Hollywood, so does she now entice us from beyond time, giving permission for sexual pleasure rather than forgiveness for sins of the flesh.

Robert Rauschenberg has been creating culturally evocative works throughout his career. Two lithographs by Rauschenberg in which Marilyn plays an important part—*Test Stone #1* (p. 67), created in 1967, and *Marmont Flair*, produced in 1991—comprise differing interpretations of the cultural context. In the earlier work,

ANONYMOUS WAS A WOMAN

Margaret Harrison (b. 1940). *Anonymous Was a Woman: From Rosa Luxemburg to Janis Joplin.* 1977. Mixed media, 43 x 112" and 12 x 96".
Courtesy of the artist and Ronald Feldman Fine Arts, Inc., New York.

Robert Arneson (1930–1993). *Elvis.* 1978. Conté crayon and pastel on paper, 40 x 30".
Courtesy of Frumkin/Adams Gallery, New York.
Robert Arneson (1930–1993). *Elvis.* 1978. Glazed ceramic, 47½ x 31 x 18⅞". Collection of the Hirshhorn Museum and Sculpture Garden,
Smithsonian Institution; gift of The Sydney and Francis Lewis Foundation, Richmond, Virginia, 1985.

Frank Xerox (b. 1959). *Almost a Frank Xerox.* 1992. F.X. mix, 30 x 30".
Courtesy of the artist.

Andy Warhol (1928–1987). *Four Marilyns*. 1967. Screenprint, 12½ x 12½".
Collection of Robert Pincus-Witten and Leon Hecht, New York.

He seemed to say it all. I'm not sure about Jesus dying for our sins, but Elvis certainly died up to his eyeballs in all this stuff, a true martyr to the normal person. He's no corporation, organization, or politician; he's human, vulnerable. I tried to paint the white suits, so godlike but with all the other bits thrown in. Elvis crucified. . . Being in America doing Elvis paintings doesn't seem so strange.
Alexander Guy

Alexander Guy (b. 1962). *Crucifixion.* 1992. Oil on canvas, 82 x 96".
Collection of Glasgow Art Gallery and Museum.

In being an artist and thinking about Elvis I thought, why not paint him the way people actually think and see him in their hearts and minds? With a paint brush I decided to put that into a reality. He was a humble man yet great; he was the King.
Rena LaCaria

Rena LaCaria (b. 1948). *Elvis the King.* 1989. Oil on canvas, 96 x 72".
Courtesy of the artist.

a passive Marilyn appears as an uninvolved deity who looks away while men involved in a variety of sports rush upward and away from her. In *Marmont Flair*, her more active expression is juxtaposed against piercing glances of Native Americans, suggesting a transformation from historical victims to powerful symbols of a phoenix-like ascendancy.

Gold Bar (p. 41) by Brooklynite Jessica Diamond is an abbreviated critique of the economic values of Americans as well as an expression of the culture's high regard for both Elvis and material wealth. The legend of Elvis, from his radical, inspired beginnings to his painful and weary last months, is almost analogous to the economic history of the United States during the last half of the twentieth century. The gold bullion shape and its visual associations with Fort Knox also contain unavoidable echoes of the Midas myth. Is Elvis the ultimate American capitalist sacrifice? Can the people who accurately identify Elvis as a sacrificial lamb through their participation in the sanctification process also be acting as economic forecasters?

In *Frog Elvis: The Lounge Act* (p. 115) by artist David Gilhooly, Elvis is playfully rendered as a green frog and performs in his hallmark white jumpsuit. The active stance is a humorous parody of Elvis' early 1970s performances, in which his stage gestures were patterned after karate movements. Initially, the homely frog seems a contrast to the handsome Elvis. There is more, however, beneath this Western fairy tale of the frog as prince. Gilhooly's sensitivity to Eastern philosophy—specifically, Buddhism—and its far-reaching influence on California life surfaces within this work. The Buddha taught that enlightenment was to be found not only in the most splendid, but also the humblest of nature's creations. Over time frogs became one of the symbols for this concept. Gilhooly's use of the frog, then, is a conflation of Eastern philosophy and Western culture and makes an analogy between the frog and Elvis' humble beginnings.

The next division of works describes Elvis and Marilyn as heroes. The works are evidence of a shift of emphasis away from the reality of their lives into the realm of legend. In *Elvis Was a Real Man* (p. 44) by South Carolina artist Kata, Elvis becomes a role model, a typical function of all mythic heroes. Here he appears preeminently masculine as he prepares to wash a sink full of dirty dishes, serving as a new exemplar of our expectations about gender roles.

Anonymous Was a Woman: From Rosa Luxemburg to Janis Joplin (p. 28) by Margaret Harrison, a feminist artist from England, stands as a memorial to famous female figures in history whose profiles reveal them to be overtly or unwittingly in the front lines of feminism and whose circumstances re-create them as heroines after death. The lives of such women as Janis Joplin, Bessie Smith, Rosa Luxemburg, and Marilyn Monroe underscore not only their unfortunate lives as a result of cultural martyrdom or discrimination, but also the trials of heroic women, both current and historical, whose names will never be known.

A desert strewn with heroic figures from different cultures in Paul Karabinis' *Elvis in the Desert* (p. 45) is a demonstration of the heroic figure as a cultural construction. Comparative heroic stature is the overt theme in this work, with the head of Elvis indicating his preeminent standing among the other figures. The identities of the other figures are keys to deeper meanings of this work. The standing figure is a Kouros, an ancient Greek statue of a youth that presided as a memorial figure over graves. Elvis is a comparable and powerful symbol of youth by virtue of his association with early rock-and-roll music, his legendary youthful good looks, and his reckless abandon on stage. The ancient Greek god of the sea,

Proteus, is here a germane figure, as his presence signals the process of change. In this category of cultural heroes, Robert Arneson's work *Elvis* (p. 29) is the consummate statement on heroic stature. Its form, the traditional Roman bust by which numerous state leaders' portraits were rendered, is infused with Arneson's wry wit and irony. The winged guitar references the winged horse Pegasus, who was the vehicle of the muses and a source of poetic inspiration; his characteristic sneer says "I told you so;" and the rock on his shoulder is a humorous inversion of the phrase "chip on one's shoulder" as well as a reference to rock and roll. This bust speaks of the good nature and practical jokes for which Elvis was known and the irony with which Elvis would have regarded his own elevation to the heroic realm.

The third category, androgyny, is the most startling state of change. As Elvis becomes softer and Marilyn more authoritative, such sexual and psychosexual

Kathleen Kondilas (b. 1948). *Madonna & Child.* 1993. Mixed media, 14 x 10½".
Courtesy of the artist.

Marc Solomon Dennis (b. 1959). *Study of Severed Elvis Head with Salmon.* 1993.
Oil on canvas, 28 x 34". Courtesy of the artist.

Calum Colvin (b. 1961). *The Two Ways of Life*. 1991. Cibachrome print, 16 x 20".
Courtesy of Salama-Caro Gallery, London.

Mimmo Rotella (b. 1918). *Marilyn Monroe.* 1962. Decollage, 77⅜ x 55½".
Courtesy of the artist. © Mimmo Rotella/VAGA, New York 1994.

Deborah Kass (b. 1952). *Double Double Yentl*. 1992. Silkscreen and acrylic on canvas,
72 x 144". Courtesy of Jose Freire Fine Art, Inc., New York.

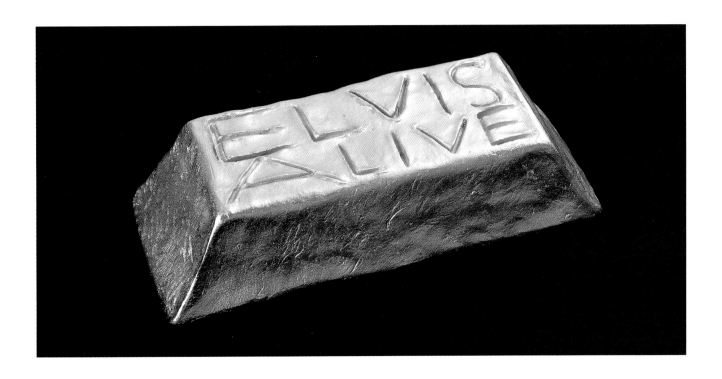

Jessica Diamond (b. 1957). *Gold Bar*. 1989–90. Gold-plated bronze, 2½ x 6⅜ x 1⅜".
Courtesy of the artist.

ambiguity provides a compelling bridge between the physical and spiritual and between the category of culture and that of its more elevated context, religion. Like mythological figures, androgynous depictions of Elvis and Marilyn are simultaneously mysterious and powerful, repugnant and irresistible, transcendent and stoic.

In *Elvis the King* (p. 33) by West Virginia artist Rena LaCaria, androgyny conveys the essence of physical vulnerability through the tentative posture of a young nude Elvis. He appears comparatively small for the grand throne on which he is poised. The muscular body underscores Elvis' mythological sexual potency while the tentative posture belies an alluring femininity. Here is Elvis in equal measures of male and female—tender and tough, a youthful king with magical powers. Underlying this androgyny lies an art historical discourse with painters whose artistic feats have attained mythic proportions. Elvis' sinewy, contorted limbs are reminiscent of El Greco's figures; the grandness of scale, the lush environment, and the festooned throne allude to Titian; the disproportionate hand and foot remind us of Michelangelo.

Warhol's *Marilyn* (p. 53) is subtly androgynous owing to its darker psychological content. At first glance, Marilyn's smile seems to indicate pleasure and abundant sexuality. Further contemplation reveals a carnivorous quality, alluding to the concept of vagina dentata and psychological castration. Additionally, a viewer who is familiar with Warhol's manipulation of his physical appearance, including cosmetic surgery to refine his nose and his bleached and teased hair, will recognize Warhol's emulation of Marilyn's image.

Frank Xerox, who resides in London, creates quotations of masterworks from a medium made from an original recipe. In his work *Almost a Frank Xerox* (p. 31), the combination of plaster and acrylic paint resembling blobs of cake icing mask any traces of Marilyn's sexuality. A dripping sentimentality, associated with images like mass-produced portraits of clowns, implies the cover-up of secret personal tragedies and a fear of acknowledging their existence. Just as Rena LaCaria has quoted masters of past centuries, so Xerox quotes unforgettable images from his own century: the indelible layers of images we see in his work include Andy Warhol appropriating Hollywood's Marilyn, Andy Warhol as Marilyn, Frank Xerox taking Andy Warhol's image of Marilyn, Frank Xerox's name as a pun on the European copier distributor Rank Xerox, Frank Xerox quoting himself, and Frank Xerox recycling press release copy to serve as a statement about his own work. The layers of meaning emanate from the canvas. His humorous comment on appropriation spoofs the concept of copyright and image ownership.

In the three untitled pieces by Keith Haring (p. 127), eyes from Hollywood photography of Elvis and Marilyn stare out of painted facades. Both have lost the charged sexuality that made them famous. Paint applied like make-up suggests Elvis' effeminacy and vulnerability, while a heavy jawline gives Marilyn's face an uncharacteristically masculine strength. Haring transforms them with his own aesthetic identity just as a viewer might overlay his or her interpretation of Elvis or Marilyn's image with his or her own sexual, personal, and cultural identity.

Jeff Way, who lives and works in New York City, creates a conflation of Elvis and Marilyn resulting in a portrait of a psychological androgyne. The dark purple background of *Idol II* (p. 94) is also a description of the mysterious moment of change. Elvis and Marilyn become a fused embodiment of transformation that is both terrifying and exciting.

The fourth group of works indicates the existence of ritual or religion. While androgyny is a physical expression of change in Elvis and Marilyn, evoking ritualistic modes of art signifies change on a religious level. These artists have borrowed historical iconography, synthesized traditional and new religious devices, utilized hieratic composition, constructed altars and shrines, or turned to symbolic materials and colors to represent Elvis and Marilyn as religious icons.

Traditionally, altars and shrines have been the focus of religious rituals of worship, sacrifice, and prayer. In *Altar to Self-Indulgence and Decadence* (p. 21) by the eastern Tennessee collaborative artists Heather and Michael Martin-Daniels, a wooden altar made from a shipping crate implies that this construction has been designed to travel. It is reminiscent of the small wooden icon boxes used in the Eastern Orthodox Church. Within the central panel resides the figure of Marilyn, whose Day-Glo scream of a halo proclaims her a Madonna, while her dress and posture stigmatize her a whore. The boastful display of her body delights Marilyn, while behind her, masses of movie extras clamber over one another in the throes of an hysterical adulatory orgy. The left panel is awash with a prancing dance chorus of headless bodies sporting fishnet stocking-covered legs. On the right panel appear symbols of arch conservatism—the pope and a manikin dressed as a monarch. A "holy" text of rock lyrics marches across the altar in a brassy declaration of the individual's right to excessive pleasure, in opposition to the virtues of modesty, servitude, and submission.

The appearance of a miracle is evidence of spiritual transformation in Dutch artist Henk Tas's *Home* (p. 46). The weeping bust of Elvis refers to Catholic statuary brought from Spain to Central and South America by missionaries. Such polychrome statues possess tears that at moments of special faith are said to glisten. The downward gaze suggests an ascended deity or Christ on the cross. Another synthesis, that of traditional Eastern philosophy and Western popular culture, exists between the Buddhist concept of transcendent awareness represented by the television/usnisha and contemporary society's habit of substituting television for the ancient tradition of meditation to achieve tranquility. The synthesis between traditional Buddhist and Christian iconographies and popular culture are visible indicators of change. The reference to historical symbolism maintains the religious context, while popular culture provides a focal point for associating religious rites with a newly emerging icon. Religious invocations exist in the overlay of a Byzantine image in

Since Elvis' image commands respect, I decided to paint him in a kitchen, cleaning a sink full of dishes, in hopes of inspiring men to do more housework.
Kata

Kata (b. 1958). *Elvis Was a Real Man.* 1993. Acrylic on canvas, 24 x 24".
Courtesy of the artist.

Paul Karabinis (b. 1952). *Elvis in the Desert*. 1993. Rephotographed collage; salted paper print from paper negative, 14 x 17".
Courtesy of the artist.

Henk Tas (b. 1949). *Home*. 1991. Color photograph/mixed media, 48 x 38⅜".
Courtesy of Torch Gallery, Amsterdam.

Edward Ruscha (b. 1937). *The King's Crown.* 1993. Dry pigment and acrylic on paper, 30 x 22½". Courtesy of the artist.

Kathleen Kondilas' *Madonna and Child* (p. 36). The Madonna's beatific three-quarter profile, with its intent gaze directed at the child, contrasts dramatically with the confrontational full face of Marilyn that emerges from the layer beneath. This superimposition of identities reveals the process of change, especially in terms of feminine gender roles. Marilyn's confident expression gives permission to let go of the traditional female occupations of motherhood and caretaker that the Madonna represents.

Alexander Guy, born in Scotland and now working in London, conflates the death of Christ with the death of Elvis in *Crucifixion* (TK). This work suggests that Elvis' painful life has ended in sacrifice, and streams of blood flow from his empty sleeves. The suit seems eerily inhabited; even without a body, the presence of the beloved seems palpable. This spiritual presence consecrates the beginning of Elvis' conceptual life and potential for immortality through the collective spirit.

A discussion of the role of death continues in a different direction with *Study of Severed Elvis Head with Salmon* by Marc Solomon Dennis (p. 37). This work has numerous art historical precedents, among them depictions of the severed heads of Medusa, Holofernes, and John the Baptist. The sardonic curled lip of Elvis, however, prevents unequivocal feelings of tragedy and sadness. As opposing concepts cancel one another out, ambivalence and dispassion emanate from the canvas, making for a meeting of the classical and the mundane, the comic and the tragic.

The King's Crown (p. 47) by California artist Edward Ruscha demonstrates the evocation of the icon through symbols. As the crown ascends into a deep night sky resembling blue suede, it appears simultaneously as a redolent constellation of light and a filmy apparition. It is evocative not only of Elvis but of the characteristics of enlightenment, timelessness, and mystery associated with icons.

The collection of works in *Elvis + Marilyn: 2 x Immortal* represent the concept of transformation in its numerous manifestations. It offers a window through which we may visualize the transformation of Elvis and Marilyn from mere celebrities to their elevation as cultural heroes, from mysterious physical embodiments of the concept of change to powerful, near-religious icons. Elvis and Marilyn, then, appear as contemporary titans through which we can witness social, cultural, and religious states of change.

These images also demonstrate how art can affect the future by perpetuating myths. They reveal the way in which artists function in society as shamans or seers. As Elvis and Marilyn emerge as immortals, we can understand art as being on the vanguard of the radical process of myth-making.

The collection raises issues about the levels of transformation associated with a particular moment in history. Newly emerging icons appear to be evidence of a culture's need to assess, to transform, to heal. Perhaps they indicate a search for identity of the self, one's own culture, the other, or the collective soul. Some of the art seems to support the idea that cultural values are not only passed downward from the economically empowered, but upward from the disenfranchised. These issues, among others, are intrinsic to the very process of change. Ultimately, *Elvis + Marilyn: 2 x Immortal* demonstrates art's facility to express inter- and intracultural needs, desires, variations, and similarities as continuous re-visions, while at the same time, it reveals the enduring nature of spirituality.

Joseph Cornell (1903–1972). *Custodian (Silent Dedication to MM)*. 1963. Wood and paper, 17⅞ x 12⅛ x 4¹⁵⁄₁₆".
Collection of The Southland Corporation.

I say "yes" to Marilyn as the paper doll from my childhood collection who was out there and having more fun than the lovely ladylike dolls we were told to emulate.
Susan Firestone

Susan Paul Firestone (b. 1946). *It's Me, Marilyn.* 1984. Mixed media, 8½ x 11½".
Collection of Herb and Rosemary Seidner, Cincinnati.

Peter Blake (b. 1932), *Marilyn Monroe Wall No. 2.* 1990. Mixed media on plywood, 66¼ x 43½".
Collection of the artist, courtesy Waddington Galleries, London.

Justin McCarthy (1892–1977). *Marilyn Monroe*. c. 1974. Acrylic on Masonite, 23½ x 15⅝".
Collection of Dr. Nancy Karlins Thoman, New York.

Andy Warhol (1928–1987). *Marilyn Monroe.* 1967. Screenprint, 36 x 36".
Collection of Judith Goldberg Fine Art, New York.

I chose a photograph of Marilyn that shows her character in transition. She is still Norma Jeane on the way to becoming Marilyn Monroe. Her hair is still soft. It curled and flowed along with my airbrush. In the future it would become brittle, brassy, and yellow. Her mouth is beginning to look plastic but has not yet firmly set. Her eyes retain a touch of softness, innocence, and hope. I painted her still in the realm of her dreams, floating between a luminous rainbow and a glossy, luscious red lipstick, one of the vehicles she used to create her magic.
I chose to paint the candle still burning to symbolize the idea that although she might have burnt out, her flame remains alive.
Audrey Flack

Audrey Flack (b. 1931). *Marilyn: Golden Girl.* 1978. Oil over acrylic on canvas, 48 x 62".
Collection of Debra and Robert Waxman, Hamilton, Ontario.

Jean Jacques Lebel (b. 1936). *Taking a Real Good Peek at Marilyn's Amazing Offer: Mass Produced Like All Show Biz's Ice Cubes in the Shapes of Luscious Nudes.*
1961. Mixed Media, 19¾ x 25¾". Courtesy of Galerie 1900-2000, Paris.

MARILYN, WE HARDLY KNEW YOU

Kate Millett

It wasn't till
they killed her that they understood. Up to that point they were perfect-
ly content with their bimbo, their pinup, their
dumb blond. That she aspired in her art, that she was
a brilliant comedienne, that she knelt before Lee
Strasberg and left him half her estate in homage—never
entered the picture. Marilyn was meat. Till she was dead meat.
The most significant element in her death was that she died naked.
That's how they saw her. The whole bunch of them, even the
women. I, too—an adolescent at the moment of her death and for that
instant at one with my culture. One gasped . . . naked. One imagined—
no, one *saw* the corpse. Dressed only in that magnificent skin.
Gradually the voyeurs relented . . . but it took a while.
Hadn't they made her a slut, sacrificed her to the lock-
er-room door, subsumed her into a collective mastur-
batory fantasy? The generic whore of an entire generation of men on the earth.
One looked on as a woman—or rather a woman in the
making—and admired her beauty, scarcely perceived her art
or humor, but burned with shame. As she was cheapened so were we
all—was she not the most perfect among us? That her grandeur could
be tits and ass, that her innocent good will could be derided not only
by lechery but cleverness: for they made her represent stupidity as
well as gorgeous breasts. Female inferiority incorporated in female
flesh. So that masculine ambition could assume intellectual superi-
ority even as it sated itself, able in one gesture to ravish and dis-
dain. The very stratagem that created the dumb blond, the
bimbo. How much more accommodating than earlier
Jezebels who exercised real power within their sin—
the bimbo is so stupid, so contemptible, one is
scarcely aware of the power of her carnal-
ity. It is defused, turned to plastic,
Styrofoam, a commodity,
mere paper,
the

centerfold: at the extreme edge mankind fucks a great
inflated rubber doll—harmless.
As to the living woman, she is only marginally human
because so negligible intellectually, the exploitation of her
flesh is but another way to humiliate and lord it over her, cheat or
expropriate her. A shell game; deceit rendering the effort of assault
unnecessary. You talked her into it—she was willing—she was even
hot. She giggled. You stuck it to her and she ate it up. When it's over
you remember that. That she was willing. Disgusted with the knee-
jerk automatic disgust of lust, the puritan acts fast to punish the
very assent he had manufactured. Heaping on her further
humiliation by giving her the name of whore. She will be
the more possessed through this word, belong more
utterly to her masters. Best of all, it will isolate
her from the women. There will be no suc-
cor from her own kind.
So she was used. Nearly
used up.

Growing
shaky by the end. Marilyn was
getting fired from pictures. Martin
Luther King, Jr., was at the nadir of his
career when someone shot him into eternity.
Marilyn was failing to show up sometimes, breaking
finally, hardly able to keep going. And then a hand raised
against her. Her own or another's—for the observer at the
time there was no difference. The most remarkable detail of
her death was its nudity. We never suspected foul play; suicide
was the appropriate thing, the end of the gang bang, as murder of
one kind or another is the logical outcome of pornography. She'd
"do herself in." The scapegoat itself executing the general sentence.
                    It was the predicted act, the expected thing, the inevitable
                        sacrificial denouement. Didn't Janis overdose? Didn't
                            Anne Sexton turn on the ignition in a closed garage,
                                didn't Sylvia Plath turn on the oven? Didn't

Bessie
Smith die with a quar-
ter in her hand after earning millions? Decades passed before we discovered that she was refused admission by a
whites-only hospital in the midst of a heart attack.
At the outset the fact that Marilyn Monroe was naked was
the most salient point of her death. This detail. That dying—that
at her last moment and in her most desperate privacy—she had
surrendered herself not only to the Los Angeles police but to the
world. There were no photographs published but for the million minds
who photographed her nudity upon a bed none were necessary. The
whole world now saw her at last—stark naked.
Now they had seen everything—would they pity? Only gradually and only
after they had sated themselves, masticating on till there was nothing left but
                    the divine husk. Then they could worship it. The woman gone, the
                        human being done in and destroyed—they took a step back
                            and appropriated her as a goddess. Forever young and
                                Anglo-Saxon, eternally even if artificially blond, forever
                                    smiling with a pretended happiness about her lus-
                                    cious mouth. It is the mouth Warhol goes for, multi-
                                    plies over and over, playing upon the implications of
                                fellatio in this opened and ecstatic orifice.
                        The very fact of her suffering is excluded by the glorious
image. The anguish of her end, the loss of face, the despair of her perceived failure, the artist's own judgment against herself, surrendering,
concurring finally with the guys. The hot shots and authorities, all the
big and little Strasbergs, the sneering and envious, even actors
who would never be as beautiful and knew it. The crowded world
itself who took the image she had created—imposed upon
her, yes, but then improved upon by the comedienne until
it transcended itself—for reality. And then denied that it
was art.
The happy girl gave up. Only then could she
be forgiven. Woman made flesh,
punished and used
and derided

Marie Pobre. *Marilyn*. 1986. Oil on canvas. 40 x 30".
Courtesy of the artist.

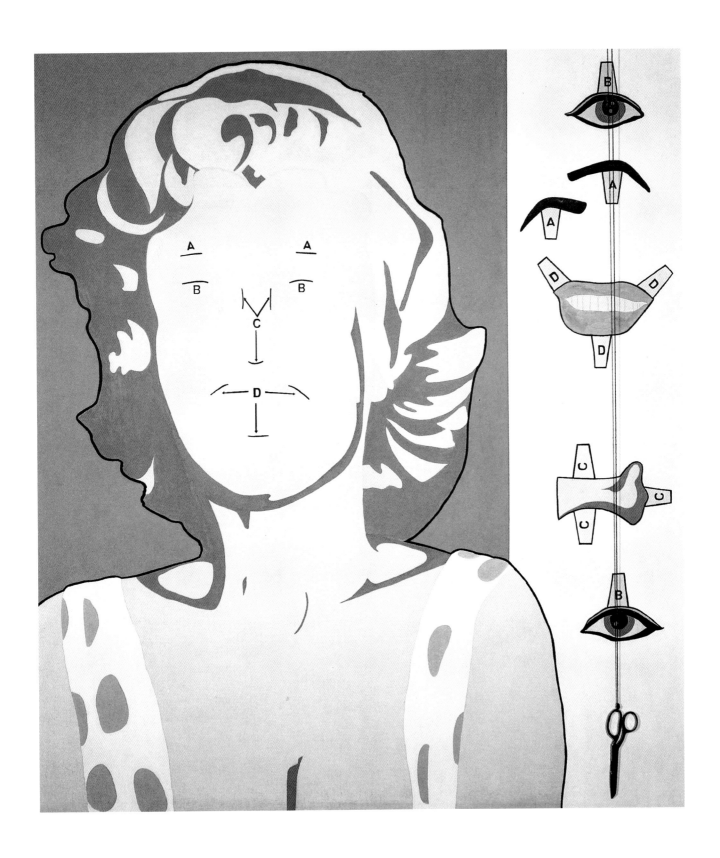

Allan D'Arcangelo (b. 1930). *Marilyn.* 1962. Acrylic on canvas with string and scissors,
60 x 55". Courtesy of the artist. © Allan D'Arcangelo/VAGA, New York 1994.

In 1961 I came upon Marilyn Found *in a trash heap outside a printing shop in lower Manhattan. It is a page sheet for* Eros *magazine featuring photographs of her by Bert Stern. What caught my eye and why I have kept it so many years were the ink smears from a maladjusted roller over her photographs and the juxtaposition of these with the articles in the magazine. Titillating articles like "Sexercises," "The Clitoris," and "French Post Cards from an Earlier Era." It made me laugh. The whole marketing machinery had gone awry and coughed up its epitaph in a better way than anything I could imagine. I didn't know at the time it would become a true epitaph.*

Allan D'Arcangelo

Allan D'Arcangelo (b. 1930). *Marilyn Found.* 1962. Found object and Plexiglas,
52½ x 40½". Courtesy of the artist. © Allan D'Arcangelo/VAGA, New York 1994.

Joseph Cornell (1903–1972). *Marilyn Monroe Source Materials,* 1955–1962. Newspaper and magazine clippings. Joseph Cornell Study Center, The National Museum of American Art, Smithsonian Institution, gift of Mr. and Mrs. Edward Batcheller.

Pruitt-Early (Rob Pruitt [b. 1965] and Jack Early [b. 1964]). *Artworks from the Private Life of Pruitt-Early (Jack Early Plays a Crazed Fan in the Cult Film, Based on* Elvis Presley The Living Legend*).* 1993. Photographic C-print mounted on stretched canvas with paper additions, 44 x 62". Courtesy of the artists.

I have always been obsessed with Elvis, not for his music but for his inner torment. Perhaps it is through the tears of our icons and idols we gain hope and possible deliverance from our own sorrow.
Carol Robison

Carol Robison (b. 1962). *Crying Icons.* 1992. Mixed media, 96 x 96".
Courtesy of the artist.

as mindless, cunt without intel-
lect. But now she would be exalt-
ed as she had once been
abased. Marilyn became desire.
Resurrected she was still denied
a mind but at last given a soul.
Dead and no longer available to
the lust of here and now in physical time, she was availability itself
for all time. Muted. Softened.
Sentimentalized. A picture.

But then she was always a picture: the photographed Marilyn—
always a still, iconography sedu-
lously avoiding the moving image
of her actual work in cinema. The myth concentrates upon the still of her mouth or the still of her skirt blown up over the
subway grating, its fabric billowing over the exhaust and revealing her thighs, then possibly her underwear, her panties and
her private parts—a prospect relished as if were to be but one more cruel joke on the dumb broad. That she enjoyed it
herself, grins in amusement and delighted complicity not only with her colleague the photographer but the world—splendid
in her conscious joie de vivre—is taken as only further evidence of her silliness. Didn't she speak in a childish voice? Wasn't
that choice itself proof? Gorgeous but not very bright. That husky simper, that very softness of timbre simply proof that she
is merely a child woman within a woman's body, a nincompoop. Now that she was dead, not only captive and diminished
by the projected shadow wherein alive she was immured—but actually dead now too, a ghost—she was launched anew.
Day after day she changed for them. They relented. Of course the manipulation escalated, took on even more hieratic
forms, served itself upon her corpse still more relentlessly. But somewhere a muscle moved, an eye blinked and looked
askance. In realization. A sympathy entered. And the whore became sacred, holy and mysterious. Never a Madonna of
course—because she was too
fun-loving and secular, too brash
altogether, and though humble—
even humiliated—she was too
pagan and happy, too sensual for
the blue mantle and the lowered
eyes of Christian feminine sub-
servience. But there was yet
something in her now of having
suffered, of tragedy. Of course
she always laughs in the picture—
sorrow is the missing element one
must bring to it. But the generation that immolated her recalls.
Those to come will already know

Peter Phillips (b. 1939). *For Men Only—Starring MM and BB*. 1961. Oil on collage on canvas, 108 x 60".
Collection of the Centro de Arte Moderna Jose de Azexedo Perdi Gao/F.C.G., Lisbon.

Rancillac (b. 1931). *Young Marilyn.* 1991–92. Acrylic on canvas. 35½ x 35½".
Courtesy of the artist and Galerie du Centre, Paris.

Nam June Paik (b. 1932). *Memory of the 20th Century*. 1963–1994. Mixed media,
121 x 72½". Courtesy of the artist and Carl Solway Gallery, Cincinnati.

Robert Rauschenberg (b. 1925). *Test Stone # 1*. 1967. Lithograph in colors, 20 x 15".

National Gallery of Art, Washington, D.C.; gift of Gemini G.E.L. © Robert Rauschenberg/Gemini G.E.L./VAGA, NY 1994

Marilyn was once sixteen. It's a fact. I've seen the photographs. They found the negatives a few years ago and made prints. These photos were everywhere for a while. In galleries, magazines, I think they even made a book out of them for coffee tables. Marilyn: sixteen, sweet and innocent, unspoiled. With just a bit of retouching to heighten the effect. Marilyn doesn't exist here. Whenever you think you've found her, she blows a kiss and fades away.
Jef Bourgeau

Jef Bourgeau (b. 1950). *You Are the One.* 1993–94. Mixed media with video, 14 x 30 x 8".
Courtesy of David Klein Gallery.

her story and bring a ready understanding of her excellence, from the beginning they perceive her as an artist; she will not have to kill herself to prove it for them. And moreover, she has the dimension now of history, woman in her time and place: there is now no need for riddle or remorse.

The final effect, then, the myth and its content—always so at odds with the lived life, the daily actuality—is always capable of containing its explanation in some back corner—the kernel of action, the turning point within a life. The final effect reverses that which proceeds it, brings us to some new place. This is particularly so with an exemplary life, the life of an icon, a saint's life, even a secular saint. One looks around at the usual and familiar impressions. Not the Madonna surely—there is no child for one thing. Not Kwannon[1] either, that great image of the Eastern world, serene goddess of mercy: single, self-contained, and in repose. There is some possible slight resemblance in their charity and kindness. But Marilyn's difference is novel: essential, of this world, resolutely sensuous, sensual, knowing. Pagan. Her laugh invites us to a pleasure we no longer need to resist nor recriminate. She has already died for our sins. The whore is sacred past the point of sacrifice because the stigma has finally been lifted. No longer a whore but a goddess, and even here she contradicts expectation; no stately Venus, but a girl who laughs: wanton, with a sense of humor, a woman full of her own pleasure, shameless . . . even fun. At last permission is granted, the taboo is broken and lies in pieces. The pleasure principle is realized in this image; not only infinitely conscious but at last a woman. Pleasure is female at last: female pleasure.

The road was so hard and it has taken so long. But here we are. After such obloquy and mortification. The character of O in *The Story of O* became Christ through her Christlike suffering whereas her tormentors merely diminished into creeps. There, too, there was the metamorphosis of transcendence. But never Marilyn's victory. O never laughed. She is the patient Griselda in a modern bordello preaching the age-old masochistic submission even if you read it with the irony of "A Modest Proposal." In Marilyn we are finally spared that age-old hortatory abnegation. Bunkum. Hogwash. Her knowing smile dissolves it, withers it. Because Marilyn is the goddess as artist. Marilyn just wanted to be good at her craft. She never aspired to what men call virtue. Ambitious as Faust but as dedicated to vitality as Eve, a suicide and still the life principle. And having been deified as sexuality itself, she turns the tables by condoning all pleasures finally for all of us.

From the far Pleiades does a star look down and approve the product despite all the elaborate machinations of the media machine, this inversion of its intended purpose her own achievement, her sleight of hand? Troilus looked back to earth and forgave every betrayal of his former life. Why not, after all? If Marilyn died to redeem us of our "hangups" (the sexual repression, guilt, and shame of a desperate patriarchy), so much the better—these were the very obstacles that stood in the way of her art inside a rape culture that denied the validity of her life's work, that careful construct which accepted its role in order to mock and overturn it.

Ultimately there is no stopping her, even the last-ditch exhortation of pornographic subterfuge melts before her humor. Pornography cannot withstand that grin. Women don't grin in that world; they are not permitted that much consciousness, that much inner presence. Even Marilyn had to die before she achieved this, was conceded it; dying probably out of sheer frustration at the tenacity with which it was withheld. Those who denied it never acknowledged her until it was too late, and so the insult was never withdrawn nor atoned.

Marilyn—we hardly knew you—even your sisters turned away. How much greater our astonished indebtedness for what you have given us in death. . . a license to live. We could be proletarian without apology, vulgar with elegance, we could be sexy, sexual. A new dispensation, an unfamiliar courage, the sassiness to carry on undaunted, a strange new immunity from all the persecution of the past.

Buster Cleveland (b. 1943). *Pop Up*. 1991. Mixed media, 21¼ x 19¾ x 2".
Courtesy of Gracie Mansion Fine Art, New York.

John Stezaker (b. 1949). *Untitled.* 1993. Collage, 23½ x 16½".
Courtesy of the artist and Salama-Caro Gallery, London.

I first came to photographing Elvis impersonators because I like making portraits of people as they imagine them-selves to be in their innermost selves, rather than in their presence in everyday life. Becoming Elvis is a fantasy lived out. There are now so many that share this fantasy that it has almost become a secret society. When I was young Elvis was my teen idol. I was the only one of my crowd who had all his records, which were played over and over again. He was the sparkle in the party in the basements of friends' houses and the church. Like most Elvis fans, he infiltrated my soul with his music and sexuality early, and I have never found another male musician who could come close to touching that part of me. If imitation is the sincerest form of flattery, keeping alive a collective dream memory is the sincerest form of love.
Patty Carroll

Patty Carroll (b. 1946). *Wall of Elvises.* 1993–94. Photographic C-prints and cibachrome, three pieces total 80 x 144".
Courtesy of the artist.

Bruce Heller and Alan C. Elms

ELVIS PRESLEY: CHARACTER AND CHARISMA

In spite of the many obvious differences between Elvis and Marilyn, there are also remarkable similarities between these two American icons. They were both supreme heartthrobs of the fifties. They shared many characteristics: their paradoxical mixture of power and fragility, of control and vulnerability; their aliveness and sexual allure; their combined hurt child/adult god(dess) persona; their fabled promiscuity, which may have arisen more from a desire to be nurtured than from directly sexual needs; their dysfunctional family backgrounds; their rise from poverty and liminal social status to dizzying heights of success and fame; their isolation from real life and their alienation from their true abilities by hosts of handlers, press agents, media moguls, and hangers-on; their failure to fulfill their initial promise; their loneliness and bouts of depression; their rejection and abandonment by those they loved; their ultimate rejection of their fame, their personae, and their core selves; their premature deaths through drug overdoses; the continuing fascination of the public with their deaths, accompanied by feelings of ambivalence or irresolution about their true character; and their sustained life-after-death in books, magazine articles, and newspapers, in allusions to them in the visual media, in their hosts of imitators, and in multitudes of rumors among the general population. While Marilyn has not, to our knowledge, been sighted in parking lots, supermarkets, or fast-food outlets, her image remains as pervasive on film and elsewhere as Elvis' voice does on recordings.

Our focus is on Elvis. What about Elvis made him—still makes him—so attractive, so compelling? As psychologists interested in the sources of charisma, we have learned to look both at what the charismatic individual offers and at the needs of those who respond

so strongly. From the beginning of his career, audience response to Elvis was extraordinary. The emotional intensity, physical activity, and sheer numbers of his fans brook few comparisons. Normally quiet and well-behaved adolescents, especially females, exploded with orgasmic abandon at the mere sound of Elvis' voice—not to mention at the crook of his finger or the wiggle of his pelvis. They screamed at his television appearances, they streamed to his films, and they bought his records by the millions. Especially during his live performances, they loosed their emotions so totally that they often seemed out of control. Ralph J. Gleason, a popular music critic for the San Francisco *Chronicle*, described a concert in Oakland in 1956: "He'd slap his crotch and give a couple of bumps and grinds and half grin at the insane reaction it produced each time. It was the first show I'd seen that had the true element of sexual hysteria in it."[1]

These responses to Elvis were unexpected, unbidden, and unbridled, as well as highly contagious. The fans' emotions and motions were not willed; they just happened—most often in Elvis' presence, but also while listening to his records. The reactions were experienced as sexual by some, and/or spiritual by others, and/or maternal by still others. But however experienced, they arose from a felt connection, a shared context, between each individual and Elvis. An articulate fourteen-year-old's response to her first Elvis concert is representative of this reaction:

I was sitting in the front row, frozen to my seat. Then he started to sing with that deep, exotic voice. "You Ain't Nothin' But a Hound Dog," he sang, pointing his finger straight at me. That was all it took to get me jumping up and down in my seat, screaming as long and loud as I could. I can't explain exactly why I acted this way, for I had never acted like this before. A woman next to me told me to be quiet, but how could I when the real Elvis Presley was right in front of me? People were pushing and yelling but all I could see and hear was Elvis and that was all that mattered.[2]

Often the excitement and intensity of feeling among so many individuals at an Elvis concert rose to such a pitch that a critical mass was exceeded, and the fans tried as one body to get closer to their ideal—physically as well as psychologically. One of the most striking incidents of this sort occurred in Jacksonville, Florida, in 1956. Elvis was using a flatbed truck as a stage and a house trailer as a dressing room. The fans rushed him when he went from stage to trailer; when he got inside the trailer, the fans rocked it until he came out, then they rushed him again. They tore the clothes off his body, leaving him only his pants. His father, Vernon, a witness to the scene, said later that he was afraid Elvis was about to be killed. Vernon compared the crowd to an out-of-control lynch mob.[3]

Cecilia Stanford (b. 1947). *Clint, Me, and Elvis.* 1992. Mixed media, 55 x 32 x 11".
Courtesy of the artist.

Alexis Smith (b. 1949). *Jailbait*. 1988. Mixed media, 42¼ x 30⅝ ". Collection of Anne and William J. Hokin;
Courtesy of Margo Leavin Gallery, Los Angeles.

When Elvis himself was asked if he had ever been seriously hurt in such a situation, he said, "Yeah, I've been scratched and bitten and everything. I just accept it with a broad mind because actually, they don't intend to hurt you. It's not that. They just want pieces of you for souvenirs, that's all."[4]

Later in his career, Elvis kept a copious supply of scarves on stage during his concerts and substituted these for pieces of himself as souvenirs. As his audience clamored and supplicated him for more, he would drape a scarf around his neck and then, when it was suffused with his sweat, would toss it into the forest of uplifted arms. In this way, we suggest, he sought to satisfy his fans' desire for a concrete token that would symbolize and cement their identification with Elvis.[5]

Elvis' magic was not just a product of the overactive glands of mid-1950s adolescents. His career hit several peaks and valleys, during which he might be said to have repeatedly died and been reborn, both personally and professionally. But for large numbers of fans, the magic never went away. Even grossly overweight, profoundly emotionally labile, and so stoned on various medications that he seemed to have difficulty talking or remembering the words to his favorite songs, Elvis remained a tremendous draw in every part of the country. Almost every performance of his last concert tour in 1977 was sold out. Many contemporary reviewers, critics, students of popular culture, and even American presidents—from Jimmy Carter to Bill Clinton—have commented on Elvis' widespread and intense presence. His sustained and indeed still-growing presence as a musical figure and cultural icon bears this out. One contemporary critic, reviewing the documentary film *This Is Elvis*, described the early Elvis as if she were still experiencing the same appeal a quarter-century later:

[T]he nineteen year old rockabilly singer Elvis Presley has a ducktail pompadour, long sideburns, and a young, hot redneck swagger; his lids are heavy and his expression is provocative—smoldering, teasing. It's the mid-fifties, and he gives country music and Negro rhythm-and-blues songs a lightning-bright attack and a frenzied fast beat. You can see his eagerness to shock people and deliver the message: good times, pleasure. His lips curl in a half grin as he gyrates; his sexual energy is like laughter busting out because it can't be held in anymore. He enjoys the impudence; it's part of the music—the new part, what's going to get a generation jumping.[6]

Negative reactions to the early Elvis' charisma also abounded; feelings ran high on both sides of the fifties' cultural divide. While masses of young people loved him, the adult establishment was less than ecstatic. Church leaders excoriated Presley and his voodoo of frustration and defiance. To them, he was a "whirling dervish of sex."[7] Tradition-bound disk jockeys burned thousands of Elvis records to show their disapproval of him and his music. District attorneys, police officials, educators, and editorialists attributed teenage violence and crime to Elvis' influence. Even *Pravda*

trumpeted that Elvis was the culmination of Western decadence.
Fan reaction to Frank Sinatra in the
1940s and to Johnnie Ray in the early
1950s had foreshadowed the emotional
response to Elvis, though in neither case
did it approach the intensity or sustained
adoration exhibited by Elvis fans. After Elvis,
however, came the deluge. He synthesized
and codified the style and thus made possible
the modern rock star, as well as a whole series
of related cultural changes supportive of such
stardom. Yet even today, forty years after Elvis
burst on the scene, few other performers are in his
league. Add the continuing sales of his music, numbers of imitators, citations in books and films, sightings in real life, and musical and cultural influence, and
 no one is. He was, and remains, the King.
  How can we account for Elvis' enormous and enduring
    popularity? In particular, why was Elvis so successful?
    At the time, there were many other young singers who
      were moving toward the synthesis of gospel, rhythm
        and blues, pop, and country music that was to become
          rock and roll. How could Elvis, having grown up in a poor
            white southern subculture, appeal so strongly to the larg-
              er mainstream culture? We begin an exploration of these
                questions by briefly recounting and analyzing Elvis' per-
                  sonal history.

ELVIS, GLADYS, AND VERNON

Elvis' relationship with his mother was the most important
of his life. He was an only child, the survivor of twins,
whose mother adored him. Mrs. Faye Harris, a neighbor in
East Tupelo, Mississippi, later commented:

> *Gladys thought he was the greatest thing that ever hap-
> pened and she treated him that way. She worshipped that
> child from the day he was borned to the day she died. She'd always keep him at
> home, or when she let him go play, she always was out seeing about him, making
> sure he was all right. . . . She wouldn't go nowheres without Elvis. Elvis'd get out of
> her sight and you could hear her hollerin' and cryin' and carryin' on to plumb down
> here, afraid he'd get lost or something.[8]*

From his birth to her death, Elvis remained the center of Gladys Presley's adulatory but
anxious and controlling attention. For example, she started walking him to school every
day when he was five—an appropriate practice at the time, since the Presleys lived on the
other side of a highway from the nearest school. But she continued to walk Elvis to school—
or at least tagged along behind him and his friends—until he was fifteen!
Elvis did not always recall this maternal concern in a positive fashion. In one interview he stated, "My mama never let me out of her sight. I couldn't go down to the creek with the other kids.
Sometimes when I was little I used to run off. Mama would whip
me, and I thought she didn't love me."[9] And in another:

> *My mother, I suppose because I was an only child I was a little
> closer, I mean, everyone loves their mother, but I was an only
> child and my mother was always with me. . . . I used to get very
> angry at her when I was growing up. It's a natural thing, isn't it? A
> young person wants to go somewhere, do something, and your*

Louis Lussier (b. 1960). *Elvis Shadow*. 1993. Photographic print, 68 x 50".
Courtesy of Jack Shainman Gallery, New York.

Justen Ladda (b. 1953). *Elvis Pelvis.* 1984. Mixed media, 134 x 100".
Collection of Jill Sussman, New York.

mother won't let you, and you think, well, what's wrong with me? But later on in years you find out she was right, that she was only doing it to protect you and keep you from getting into trouble and getting hurt. And I'm very happy she was kind of strict on me.[10]

In these remarks Elvis offers, in his own words, a blueprint for dysfunctional patterns of attachment between his mother and himself. He describes how Gladys reacted with punishment, increased her control, and withdrew her love when he sought to begin separating from her. He says this made him very angry as a child, though he learned later in life that she was only trying to protect him. This partial rationalization was adaptive when Elvis was small, but it became less so as the years went by. That he accepted his mother's intrusive overprotectiveness as legitimate implied that he was not like the other kids. In one way, this would have made him feel special, feeding his tendencies toward narcissism. But it also likely made him feel that something was wrong with him as he sought to individuate from his mother—that he was in need of more protection than his peers, or that it was just plain bad to worry his mother so. Thus his acceptance and rationalization of his mother's behavior promoted guilt and low self-esteem.

Gladys' hovering concern for Elvis was stimulated in part by events and circumstances surrounding his early childhood. She had probably been sensitized to them by her own experiences as a child in a highly dysfunctional family.[11] Two years before her marriage, Gladys' father died. Elvis' twin brother Jesse was stillborn. Shortly after the birth, Gladys' mother and maternal grandmother died. Elvis was born into a bitterly cold Tupelo winter, that was followed in less than a year by a massively destructive tornado that killed 235 Tupelo residents, injured 350, and destroyed a large part of the city, including a church near the Presleys' home. The economic climate was just as bleak. The Presleys were dirt-poor, living in a two-room shotgun shack without plumbing, near the black Shakerag section of Tupelo—quite literally on the wrong side of the tracks. Tupelo was an economically depressed city, within an economically depressed state, within an economically depressed region of the country, during the Great Depression.

When Elvis was almost three years old, his father Vernon, a truckdriver, Gladys' brother, and another man were arrested for altering a check from their employer, increasing it by a modest amount. The other men were released on bail, but Vernon apparently spent six months in the county jail while awaiting trial and was then sentenced to three years in the infamous Parchman State Penitentiary. He served nine months at "Parchman Farm," then was pardoned by the governor because of the hardship his imprisonment was causing his family.[12] During that time the Presleys lost their house, and of course Vernon lost his job, the best job he'd ever had. When he got out of prison he had to perform simple farm labor again. Eventually he got a WPA job some distance from Tupelo, then found employment at a defense factory in Memphis, a hundred miles away—a job that necessitated his absence from the family for most of two years, except for an occasional weekend at home. During these extended periods with the father gone, Gladys and Elvis apparently continued to share the same bed. This experience, potentiated by Vernon's absence, likely further intensified and sexualized the already strong bonds between mother and child, paving the way for future conflicts. The continued economic hardship was disruptive of family life in other ways as well. The Presleys moved repeatedly within Tupelo and later within Memphis, often living near black neighborhoods where housing was cheap and opportunities for Elvis to hear black music were rich. The Presleys were always poor, often desperately so, with little prospect that things would change, especially after an incident in which Vernon injured his back and became partially disabled. And things didn't change until Elvis started singing professionally. These repeated losses and threats of further losses during Elvis'

childhood and adolescence must
have sparked enormous anxiety in Gladys, as they only
added to her earlier experiences of physical danger and economic
distress. She appears to have responded by directing ever more controlling attention, and enormous expectations, onto her son. Such traits in Gladys'
personality would probably have found expression anyway, even if Vernon hadn't
served time, given the family's precarious circumstances and her own character structure. But the financial, social, and emotional impact of Vernon's (and her brother's)
imprisonment must have powerfully intensified Gladys' fears and feelings of neediness.
Vernon's legal troubles occurred during the time that Elvis would ordinarily have completed
the process of separation-individuation. During this stage of development, the child is born
psychologically, as distinct from its earlier biological birth.
Psychologist Margaret Mahler and her colleagues have documented this process, during which
the infant emerges from a posited symbiotic unity shared with its mother
to establish "a sense of separateness from, and relation to, a world of
reality, particularly with regard to the experience of one's own body
and to the principal representative of the world as the infant
experiences it, the primary love object."[13] According to Mahler,
the separation-individuation process involves mastering the
fear of object loss through the internalization and construction of stable, whole self- and object-representations, and the
development of pleasure in independent functioning. In her
view, it is on such mastery that all future psychological
growth depends. The process is divided into four phases. The
third phase, rapprochement, occurs between the ages of eighteen
and twenty-four months, and beyond. Here the child enjoys to the utmost his newfound
autonomy, but he also needs to be able to return periodically to a safe harbor. For
optimal resolution of this phase, the mother must be a stable object—unwound-
ed by the child's autonomous activity, available when the child returns.
All through what should have been Elvis' period of separation and
individuation from his mother, he must have experienced
Gladys' emotional neediness. Vernon's sudden and extended
absence came at a time when he might otherwise have been able to help
Elvis deal with the difficulties involved in concluding the rapprochement phase.
On the basis of Elvis' own comments, as well as aspects of his musical performances, we speculate that Gladys was unable to tolerate and encourage Elvis' phase-
appropriate attempts at exploration, individuation, and the building up of a stable sense of
relatedness. She appeared to perceive his sallies into the world as rejections,
wounding her already fragile sense of security and self-esteem, and
resulting in misattunements[14] or failures of appropriate emotional
mirroring[15] during the intricate dance of attachment. We suspect
that Elvis' attempts at psychological separation were greeted with
a withdrawal of nurturance, while his attachment behavior was
reinforced with renewed, overly intrusive nurturance. For the
young Elvis, it must have been impossible to understand the
withdrawal of his mother's love (which made him feel lonely and
bad) when he began to individuate (which felt good) or why his
mother loved him so fiercely when he returned to her that he felt
smothered (as well as very special).
Gladys' fears of loss and her probable ongoing depression also
appear to have strongly impacted the quality of the attachment
she and Elvis shared. The likely result was an attachment that
was insecure and ambivalent[16] and/or disorganized.[17] The
establishment of such a relationship pattern in childhood
would have profoundly affected Elvis' later personality development and the kinds of choices he made in terms of close personal relationships.
An important fact of Elvis' early emotional life was that he had no

There were these three guys at the Esplanade Hotel, always up front and looking like Elvis Presley. One had the side-burns, one was wearing white flares held up by a huge Elvis buckle, one was overweight, wearing an open-necked shirt and all sported beautifully manicured coifs. Then one day at a rock concert on St. Kilda Beach, in the middle of the crowd, there were the three of them, ghetto blaster pumpin' out, giving their all-time best Elvis impersonations. Thus the three Elvises were born.

Jon Campbell

Jon Campbell (b. 1961). *The Three Elvises.* 1988. Oil and enamel on canvas, two panels, each 88 ⅛ x 119 ½".
Private collection, Melbourne.

My earliest memory of Elvis Presley's music was hearing "Hound Dog" on the radio when I was about five years old. My mom was hanging clothes on the line, it was a lush Louisiana spring or summer. One of my favorites of his songs was "Heartbreak Hotel" because of the way Elvis' voice sounded like a wounded animal echoing from the bottom of a well.
Douglas Bourgeois

Douglas Bourgeois (b. 1951). *A New Place to Dwell*. 1987. Oil on wood panel, 14 x 19".
Collection of Dr. Ronald Schwarz and Ms. Ellen Johnson.

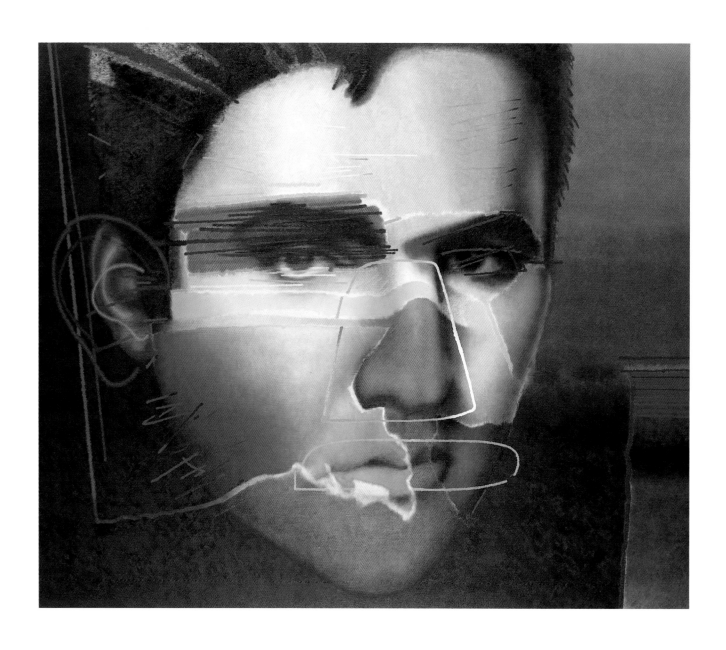

Ed Paschke (b. 1939). *Matinee*, 1987, Oil on canvas, 68 x 80".
Private collection, Chicago.

father to move to as he moved from his mother's orbit. Not only was his father mostly absent during this crucial period, he was not a very impressive role model during Elvis' later childhood and adolescence, given his blunder with the altered check and his inability to provide for his family. At the age of twenty-one, Elvis commented in a symbolically castrating way on his father's earning capacity: "I made my father retire a few months ago. There isn't much sense in his working, since I can make more in a day than he can in a year."[18]

Vernon's physical and emotional absence during much of Elvis' early childhood may also help explain Colonel Tom Parker's enormous subsequent influence on Elvis, as well as Elvis' fascination with symbols of authority, especially guns and law-enforcement badges.[19] In the Colonel, who served as his manager for most of his career, Elvis appears to have found a father figure, an authority, to replace the one he didn't have when he was young. Elvis was thus able to make a limited move from his mother to the world, from dyadic to triadic interpersonal relations. However, he also became so dependent on the Colonel that he was unable to tolerate separation from him to any great degree. After briefly breaking with Parker in 1970, Elvis impulsively flew to Washington, where on the spur of the moment he requested and received a federal narcotics agent's badge from an even more powerful authority—President Richard Nixon.[20]

As a young child, Elvis internalized Gladys' dreams and wishes as a sense of mission. As he reached adolescence, they began to affect his behavior more and more forcefully. He aspired to become somebody, to give Gladys the life Vernon was unable to give her. But as he did so, the conflict unresolved in the initial separation-individuation process reasserted itself with a vengeance. Becoming successful—individuating—at this level meant becoming a potent adult male able to commit to a mate of his own choosing. In order to do this, Elvis could not remain Gladys' baby, dependent on and loving only her the way he had done as a child. This, then, was Elvis Presley's double bind: how to become a successful, powerful, adult male, capable of autonomous functioning and mature attachments, and to remain Gladys' baby. If he were age-appropriately independent, he would fear wounding her and being abandoned; if he were to remain her baby and dependent, he would fear being engulfed and becoming developmentally stuck.

We speculate that these two aspects of Elvis' early experience became ego states, organized in an unstable, dynamic structure or configurational schema.[21] In such a structure, the experience of one ego state can lead to the other, and vice versa, in continual loops, mediated by feelings of emptiness, depressive longing, self-recrimination, and anger. Thus, when Elvis was in his child self state, he would be most influenced by his mother's injunction, "Be my baby!" The consequence of such a directive, if followed, would be that Elvis was unable to grow in developmentally appropriate ways. He would be loved only when he was dependent, vulnerable, and helpless. When he sought separation or autonomy, his mother—or his inner representation of her—would reject him. However, when he was in his grandiose self state, encouraged by his mother to "be somebody," Elvis would be unable to relate or to be intimate with others, isolated by his role and persona—although he would be loved for being successful and autonomous. In his child state, Elvis might fear

Nicholas Higgins (b. 1960). *Elvis Book 1* (detail). 1989.
Enamel on paper in cloth-bound book, 4 ½ x 6 ¼ x ½", courtesy of the artist.

Elvis died, and I don't remember, but I do remember a railway shed outside Birmingham painted
"Elvis is dead ha ha ha, 1978."
I started to pick up Elvis records. They were funny and some of them looked great. I've got the beautiful color booklets
and gatefolds from the sixties. I've also got Elvis Sings for Kids. *How could anyone have put together*
the cover for Separate Ways? *It has a huge Elvis in Vegas white floating*
supernaturally over a concrete freeway at rush hour.
Nicholas Higgins

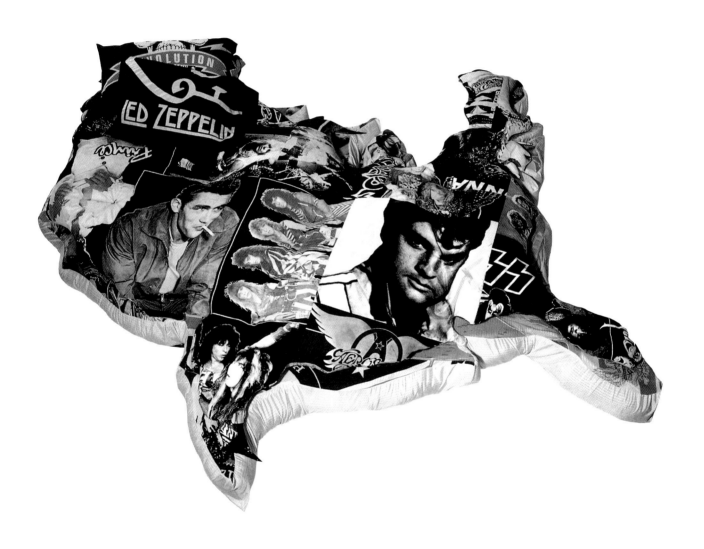

Joel Otterson (b. 1959). *The Bed from Hell.* 1988. Mixed media, 24 x 132 x 108".
Courtesy of Yokohama Museum of Art.

being either attacked and rejected or smothered; in his grandiose state, Elvis might fear being either isolated or adulated. In either state, reciprocal, satisfying interpersonal relations were impossible, and Elvis often felt disappointed, inadequate, angry, and, ultimately, profoundly depressed. We suggest that this dynamic structure, which initially grew out of his relationship with his mother, was replayed in every important relationship Elvis entered into through the rest of his life. While this core conflict resulted in high levels of energy and creativity, it was also deeply dysfunctional. Thus Elvis could never be truly happy, and his behavior became increasingly irrational.

Even though he remained a thoroughly dutiful son, as his career took off Elvis began to separate from Gladys more and more, emotionally and geographically. He also developed an increasing number of other attachments, so that although at the deepest level Gladys remained his whole world, she became visibly only a small part of it. This separation must have been very difficult for Gladys, given her controlling interest in her son and her own history of losses. She appears to have felt more and more abandoned and depressed. She ate more; she began to take diet pills; she also began to drink a good deal. Soon after Elvis left for boot camp in preparation for military service in Germany, he found a house off base to share with his parents, and he planned to have them move to Germany to remain close to him. But Gladys nevertheless seems to have perceived his submission to the military draft as a further abandonment. After Elvis had served five months in the army, and one month before his scheduled departure for Germany, Gladys became acutely ill and died.

The pull between being his mother's baby and functioning at an age-appropriate level must have been extremely difficult for Elvis. When his mother died he was devastated: "Oh God, everything I have is gone," he is reported to have said.[22] His devastation came not only from a profound sense of loss, but probably also from guilt arising both from his feelings of having abandoned her and from his unconscious anger toward her.

EMERGENT CHARISMA

How did Elvis' personal history and core conflicts lead to the supreme accomplishments he achieved, in spite of his life's ultimate tragedy? Besides his voice, movements, and musical originality, Elvis' initial appeal rested in part on his suitability as a vehicle through which adolescents could voice their rebellion against adult values. But his charismatic appeal, which extended far beyond the adolescent population, also resided in his ability to connect with his audience, to allow them to feel emotions of sadness, anger, and joy. This ability derived in part from a central aspect of Elvis' personality, his son/lover character, which was shaped by his conflicted relationship with his mother. We speculate that he was initially treated by Gladys, and came to regard himself, both as a young, dependent child and as a potent, erotic lover. Because of this early developmental history, he continually merged the inner image of his mother with those of his girlfriends, including his wife Priscilla. We have already suggested that Elvis' early childhood experiences resulted in the formation of two major self-representations in an unstable but exceedingly charming and creative personality structure—a grandiose, momentarily invulnerable, even godlike self, and a needy, vulnerable, childlike self. We hypothesize that Elvis' son/lover character—the fusion of passive, childlike, but engagingly vulnerable elements with potent, erotic, but sometimes cruel character elements—was salient in producing the paradoxical behavior patterns Elvis exhibited, as well as the frenzied emotion of his fans. Women responded to him in a dual way: they wanted to mother him at the same time that they were erotically attracted to him. It was this mixture of maternal and sexual feelings that Elvis engendered in his female fans that made him so alluring. Unfortunately, his inability to separate his feelings about his mother and his girlfriends also resulted in his unhappiness, recurrent feelings of emptiness, and ultimate decline.

In performance, Elvis' son/lover character communicated enormous aliveness and potency as well as accessibility and vulnerability. His famous smile/sneer radiated both messages: open, friendly, sensitive, yet animal, passionate, perhaps even cruel. For Elvis, women were on a conscious level either maternal or sexual objects; at a subconscious level, he responded to them as fused maternal and sexual part-objects. Women often reciprocated in the same way. Marion

Ray Johnson (b. 1927). *Marilyn Monroe's Mother's Potato Masher.* 1972/81/87.
Ink drawing and collage, 15 x 15". Collection of Rolf Nahr, Berlin.

Mike Hale (b. 1961). *King.* 1993. Acrylic on canvas, 72 x 48".
Courtesy of the artist.

Keisker, the Sun Records studio manager whose initial enthusiasm for Elvis' singing led to his early professional recordings, has provided an account consistent with this observation. She was about thirty-seven when she attended Elvis' first large concert, at the Overton Park Shell in Memphis in 1954. Note the mixture of sexual and maternal themes in her reaction:

> [T]here was such a stage presence, such fantastic ease, what's called charisma today . . . one of the songs he sang was "I'll Never Let You Go, Little Darling." He'd sung that in the studio and looked at me. Now I'm a restrained person, in public anyway, and I heard somebody screaming, just keening, and I discovered it was me, the staid mother of a son. I was standing out there screeching like I'd lost my total stupid mind.[23]

We should note that Elvis consistently treated the eighteen-years-older Keisker with respect, as he did his own mother, but that does not contradict the indications of an underlying erotic tone in their relationship.

We find evidence for the son/lover configuration especially in Elvis' early recordings, many of which incorporated words and metaphors that are both maternal and sexual. Consider, for example, "That's All Right, Mama" (1954). This song is especially significant because it was the spontaneous choice of the young, aspiring singer desperate to make good in his first professional recording session. In the song's first verse, "Mama" refers specifically to the singer's mother. In the repeated chorus and the song's title, however, Mama refers to the girlfriend who has left him and about whom his Mama had warned him.

A mixture of sexual and maternal themes is prominent in the lyrics of another early hit, "Baby, Let's Play House" (1955), the first of Elvis' recordings to make Billboard's national charts. Here the singer pleads with his girlfriend, who has rejected him and who may already be involved with another man, to return to him so that they can play house (presumably, act out adult roles and have sex) as they did before. The original, written and first recorded by Arthur Gunter, contains fourteen mentions of the word "Baby"—certainly enough for any ordinary purpose. Elvis, however, repeats the word thirty-one more times at his recording's beginning and end. This elaboration assumes greater significance in light of Elvis' use of "Baby" as a nickname for his mother. The connection between the girlfriend in the song and Elvis' mother is further strengthened by his only other change from the original version; he inserts a line describing his baby as owning a pink Cadillac. Nineteen months after Elvis released this song, he bought a pink Cadillac for his mother, although she did not drive. After she died, he kept the car as a treasured memento until his own death.

Elvis recorded the blues classic "Milkcow Blues" as "Milkcow Blues Boogie" in 1955. In the song's traditional lyrics, the cow, an obvious maternal symbol, is used as a metaphor for the singer's girlfriend, who once again has left him. The song directly combines themes of maternal resources, sexual gratification, and abandonment. At times its lamentations of abandonment are mixed with angry threats of punishment, as the singer, calling himself "Daddy," confuses sexual and parental roles. The abandoned child, the adolescent chafing under parental restrictions, the spurned adult lover, all appear to merge in the words of this fast, exultant hymn of vengeance, which sounds as though it released Elvis' emotions as they must seldom have been released before.

Let us summarize the personal characteristics contributory to Elvis' appeal, as indicated by his fans, his foes, and Elvis himself. Prominent among these are his rebelliousness, his sexuality, marginality, enthusiasm, his exceptional voice, his dress, and his energetic, erotic, and yet strangely awkward body movements. All contributed to his uncanny ability to engender joy and emotional release. Less often mentioned but nonetheless important were his politeness, accessibility, and vulnerability. Elvis was often spoken of as if he were a member of the family. Many of his fans felt, even if they had never met him, that they had a personal relationship with him. Even Ed Sullivan, who had earlier vowed that Elvis would never appear on his television show, commented during Elvis' third and last appearance that he was "decent" and "a nice person." Except for his genetic endowment— voice, looks, and the like—all the qualities we have mentioned may be subsumed under that quasi- oxymoronic construct, Elvis' son/lover character. Elvis often seemed to regard himself as others, especially women, often saw him: both as a potent, erotic demigod and as a little boy. This is not to deny that at times he caricatured himself in the erotic role, as did Marilyn. But there were many times when he took it, and himself, very seriously.

THE SOCIAL FUNCTIONS OF ELVIS' CHARISMA

The rebellious adolescent sub- culture that began to emerge during the conservative 1950s questioned the values and the authority of the mainstream cul- ture. Dissatisfaction grew because the mainstream no

Jeff Way (b. 1942). *Idol II*. 1983. Oil on canvas, 36 x 30".
Courtesy of the artist.

Ed Paschke (b. 1939). *Pink Lady 2*. 1993. Ink on paper, 37½ x 26".
Courtesy of the artist and Phyllis Kind Gallery, Chicago/New York.

longer met the needs of many Americans. This was, in Arnold Toynbee's phrase, a "time of troubles," and it gave rise to Elvis and rock and roll. Neither Elvis nor most mid-1950s young adults were political; they were instead, in the words of one of Elvis' favorite films, "rebels without a cause." But they laid the groundwork for the politically aware youth movements of the 1960s: rebels with a cause.

One element necessary for any charismatic personality's success, then, was met by social conditions in America during the 1950s: there was a great deal of strain among various segments or subcultures within and on the fringes of the mainstream culture. The young Elvis, as any charismatic leader does, epitomized and expressed values whose meaning the mainstream culture had either discarded or overlooked.[24] These values were not only different from those of the mainstream, but were also, in various regards, compensatory to its value system. Integration of these values into the mainstream proved helpful on three levels: intrapsychically (within the mind of the individual), interpersonally (among members of the subculture), and transculturally (between the small group or subculture and the large mainstream culture). The culture as a whole was thus strengthened.

It was not only Elvis' deep, exotic voice, bodily gyrations, and musical talent that were responsible for his success. As we have observed, it was also his sense of mission, his rebelliousness, his sexuality, his marginality, his intense struggles with autonomy and dependency. These emotional stances and conflicts reflected what many adolescents were feeling during the mid-fifties.

Elvis was a romantic, rebellious, sexual, lower-class outsider when he burst upon the popular music scene. He was southern and therefore perceived by many as being marginal to the mainstream culture. He was poor and therefore marginal even to the dominant southern culture. He spoke for liberation from a structure of oppressive social and sexual rigidity—both within the South and in America at large. Elvis was perceived as expressing the frustration of oppressed groups— young people, women, blacks—who also felt themselves marginal to the mainstream. Moreover, this white man singing like a black man, who mixed rhythm and blues, gospel, country, and pop styles, provided his fans with an emotional release and an experience of unmatched ecstasy, as well as intimations of a loosening and restructuring of cultural norms in a way that was not directly confrontational. As his career progressed, Elvis also epitomized the hunger these groups had for success, fame, and material things. He became the symbol of the American dream, a role that had its bright and its dark sides. Elvis as a continuing cultural icon incorporates all those characteristics.

In the 1950s, Elvis symbolized parent/child and adult mainstream/youth culture conflicts. He provided adolescents, as individuals, not only with an experience of hope and joy, but also a sense of identity, group cohesion, and meaning, a focus sorely needed by this newly emerging subculture. For the culture as a whole, he facilitated the awareness and assimilation of vital, compensatory cultural currents and a loosening of overly rigidified, overly hierarchical musical and cultural forms.

Similar themes may be traced in other cultures and other times. These themes were often linked in myth and religious ritual to the motif of the dying and rising god. The Greek god Dionysus is a prime exemplar. Both his life history and the practices of his worshipers (fans) offer striking parallels to Elvis and his most zealous devotees. When Nietzsche identified two broad cultural patterns as Apollonian and Dionysian, he was using the latter name to represent the set of cultural trends we see as most strikingly embodied in Elvis, and the name of the god Apollo to represent at least a portion of the trends prevailing when Elvis appeared on the scene. These two opposite but complementary cultural trends may

be
seen
as part
of a self-
correcting
mechanism for
cultural and indi-
vidual homeostasis
and development. Either
of the two principles may
provide corrective input
whenever the cultural pendulum
swings too far the other way.
We would not suggest that Elvis is an
archetypal representation of the rising
and dying god in the literal Jungian sense.
But the striking similarities do seem to
underline aspects of Elvis' character as
related to his audience's responses
to him. These include the god's and
Elvis' potency and aliveness (immortality); their vulnerability (dismemberment or
attempts thereof); their accessibility and
marginality (their appeal is initially to the
lower classes, rural folk, women, slaves
and/or oppressed youth); their son/lover
characters; their narcissism and preoccupation with their own mission;
the ecstasy that they inspire in
their fans and celebrants; and
finally their function as culture heroes—intermedi-
aries between the gods
(or collective soci-
ety) and humans.
The various ris-
ing and dying
gods were,
like Elvis,
agents

of personal and cultural change, renewal, and meaning. Perhaps it is not so surprising, then, that our modern culture hero, Elvis, apparently dead since 1977, seems to rise again with new sightings almost every week.[25] No other martyr of our time—not John Lennon, not John F. Kennedy, not Martin Luther King, Jr., not Malcolm X—has remained so alive in the public consciousness.

* * *

Many biographers have commented on the "mystery" or paradoxical nature of Elvis Presley's personality and life course. He was full of contrasts: a figure of magnetic sexuality on stage, who continued to live with his parents until his mother died and his father remarried; passionate and promiscuous, but diffident and chivalrous toward women in public; sensitive, tender, and easily hurt, yet with a potential for explosive violence; a white man who sang with a black man's style; a gifted musician who did not read music, write his own songs, or play the guitar very well; a prescription drug addict to whom President Nixon presented a federal drug agent's badge; a charismatic figure perceived by his fans as a demigod and as the boy next door. Elvis was a man/child with a dramatic, rebellious persona, whose origins were liminal to the cultural mainstream but who became phenomenally popular among the youth of his era and was ultimately accepted by the mainstream. His music spoke to such issues as loneliness, abandonment, and personal oppression—and by implication, socioeconomic oppression—in ways that gave his audiences a shared experience of emotional connectedness and release, an ecstasy that softened their frustrations and promised hope for change, or at least for self-renewal.

Rising from rural poverty and obscurity to enormous professional success, Elvis captured the American imagination. Yet in spite of his abilities, his opportunities, and his accomplishments, Elvis never fully realized his creative potential. He was lonely and unhappy most of his life, he failed to establish genuine long-term reciprocal relationships with men or women, and he died at age forty-two from a combination of sustained physical self-neglect and multiple drug abuse. Our psychobiographical analysis suggests that the "mystery" of his personality—under which may be subsumed his depression, erratic behavior, unstable relationships, drug abuse, physical decline, and early death—as well as his enormous musical influence and cultural impact, may be explained in part by his persistent difficulties with the basic psychological processes of attachment and separation-individuation. It was because of his developmental history and his singular abilities—his intense, repeated experience of intimacy and abandonment, combined with his unique talent in expressing his experience—that Elvis Presley became a seminal figure in contemporary American music, a cultural icon, and a psychological casualty.

Bert Stern (b. 1929). *Document.* 1962. Silkscreen, 38 x 30".
Courtesy of Renee Fotouhi Fine Art East, New York.

Of all the women I have photographed, only Marilyn Monroe possessed the uncanny quality of feminism in the flesh.
I use the word "feminism" not in its present manifestation, but in the spiritual sense.
Bert Stern

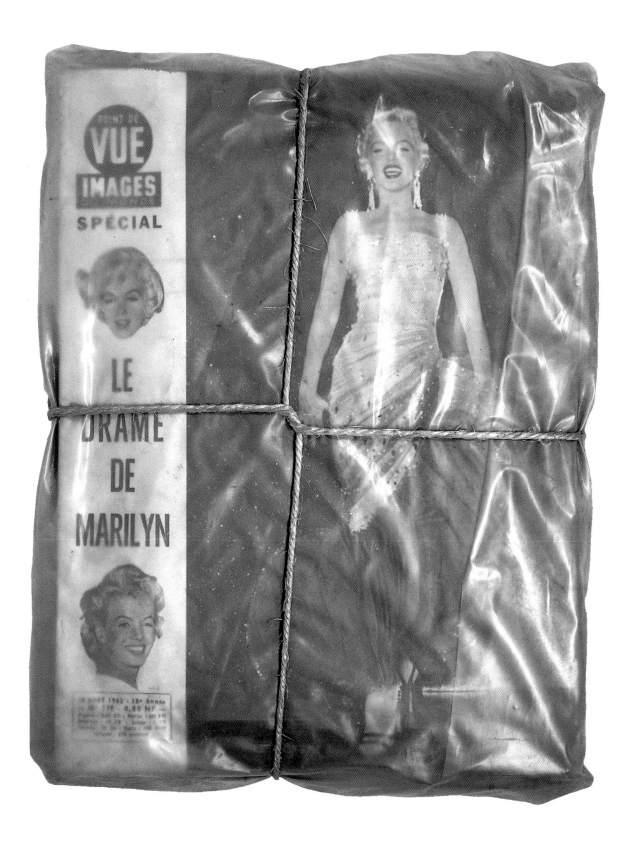

Christo (b. 1935). *Revues Empaquetées.* 1962. Magazines, plastic, and string,
14 x 11 x 1¼". Courtesy Sonnabend Collection.

Richard Hamilton (b. 1922). *My Marilyn*. 1965. Silkscreen on paper, 40⅜ x 48".
Courtesy of Sotheby's.

"Your candle burned out long before / Your legend ever did," sang Elton John of Marilyn Monroe in "Candle in the Wind." The flame of her candle was fiery in popular culture and iconology, and present in ways that we know well.

Richard Hamilton, one of Britain's foremost postwar artists, lets us see Monroe differently, if no less brightly, than in the shine of the candle. His work *My Marilyn was* created in 1965, not so long after her 1962 suicide. In it, he recasts a mediated Monroe—a figure who was then already deeply absorbed in the media intrigue of image-making—into the world of art-making. Hamilton, one of the artists most identified with the Pop art movement, mixes painterly gesture, art historical insight, and tra-

ditional fine arts skills with a keen, occasionally mischievous curiosity for mass media and film. In this work, he evolves a Marilyn of his own—even so named: *My Marilyn*—and one specific to his vision.

Critically, there is no omnibus Marilyn, no direct Marilyn, no unintervened Marilyn. Leo Braudy, a shrewd critic of fame, has written, "Monroe's iconography yokes together the mystic priestess and the woman destroyed by passion, both staples of the nineteenth- and twentieth-century operatic heroine."[1] But Braudy seeks the heroine and strives to define the common and complementary icon. Hamilton, *avant la lettre,* deconstructs the imagery, beginning with a premise in history and a predisposition to critical analysis.

Janice E. Williams (b. 1954). *Icon Series: Graces Under Fire.* 1986. Charcoal and acrylic on canvas, 34¼ x 40½".
Courtesy of the artist.

Daze (b. 1962). *Runaway*. 1989. Spray paint and acrylic on canvas, 73 x 64".
Courtesy of Modern Culture, New York.

Of
course, Hamilton's
overt comment is on
Monroe's legendary control
of her own image and media,
demanding selection rights over all
of her published photographs. Hamilton
described:

> The aggressive obliteration of her own image
> has a self-destructive implication that her
> death made all the more poignant; there is also
> a fortuitous narcissism for the negating cross
> is also the childish symbol for a kiss. My
> Marilyn *starts with her signs and elabo-*
> *rates the graphic possibilities these sug-*
> *gest.*[2]

Hamilton's proposition is deliberately
contrarian. He assumes Monroe to be
the semiotician and theoretical mark-
maker, not solely the subject of the

image.
His interest
is in seeing the
editing, determining
skill of Monroe, instead
of her customarily exploit-
ed role as the subject. In this,
Monroe is given a power she
seldom achieves in her rich modern iconography, for she is ostensibly
the manipulator, not merely the manipu-
lated.
In fact, Hamilton annuls image and specifically revokes the Monroe imagery again and
again in this work. She who was bright icon
and familiar martyr to the media by 1965 is
here voided again and again by what is the
simile of her own hand and decision. In the upper
center image, a field as clotted as a de Kooning
female of the 1940s and 1950s becomes obscure; a
veil of pointillist reproduction prevails in the lower-left
frame; and a kind of cut denies Monroe herself in the
lower right. All three are effacements of the most ordinary kind, seldom combined in one image. Hamilton
commented that this image combined its constituent

diverse images and
therefore lacked a unified perspective. The lack of unity is underscored
by the several methods of veiling, obscuring,
and camouflaging the inherent image.
Monroe explored several options in the determina-
tion of her own image. She could cross out images,
rendering them not printable by the magazine; she could
indicate cropping and other treatments of images that
would render them acceptable as emended to the subject; or
she could accept an image, as she does in the one marked
"good." Photographer Eve Arnold testified to the
process, indicating in one instance, "There were
one or two that [Monroe] felt were not quite
right, and I agreed to destroy them." That
was a photographer's acquiescence in
Monroe's own lifetime. One would have
expected Hamilton the artist to have arbi-
trated this imagery more than he has. He
abrogates his artistic right to Monroe, the
editor/image-maker, in an unusual act of
deference. Is this the historical respect and
referencing that comes from Hamilton's
understanding of Monroe's view of the
image? After all, Hamilton is the artist who
translated into English Marcel Duchamp's notes
for *The Bride Stripped Bare by Her Bachelors,
Even*—an exceptional homage to a cryptic master
who sought verbal, aesthetic, and intellectual control over his work as obsessively as Monroe
sought dominion over these images.
Has Richard Hamilton the archetypal artist-
intellectual yielded to Marilyn Monroe
the mediator, if not to the siren Monroe to whom so many others
have succumbed? Hamilton
respects Monroe's role
and   contextualizes
it without sur-
rendering
to it. Of

course, in the context of art this peremptory power of the celebrity finds analogy in the prerogatives of the artist. Thus,
Rauschenberg's *Erased de Kooning Drawing* acknowledges the
similar privilege of the modern artist, as indeed the visual artists,
certainly in the modernist and avant-garde traditions, have felt
free to represent the past as a chalkboard for contemporary
investigation and emendation. Negation and obliteration are the
artistic radicalism of the twentieth century. Can this expunging
gesture, ratcheted to the celebrity as artist, still give evidence of
the modernist impulse to *tabula rasa?* This referencing requires
us to think that Hamilton may have treated Monroe's place as
akin to that of the artist. Her sovereign selection of image and her
opportunity for continued reworking is parallel to that of the artist,

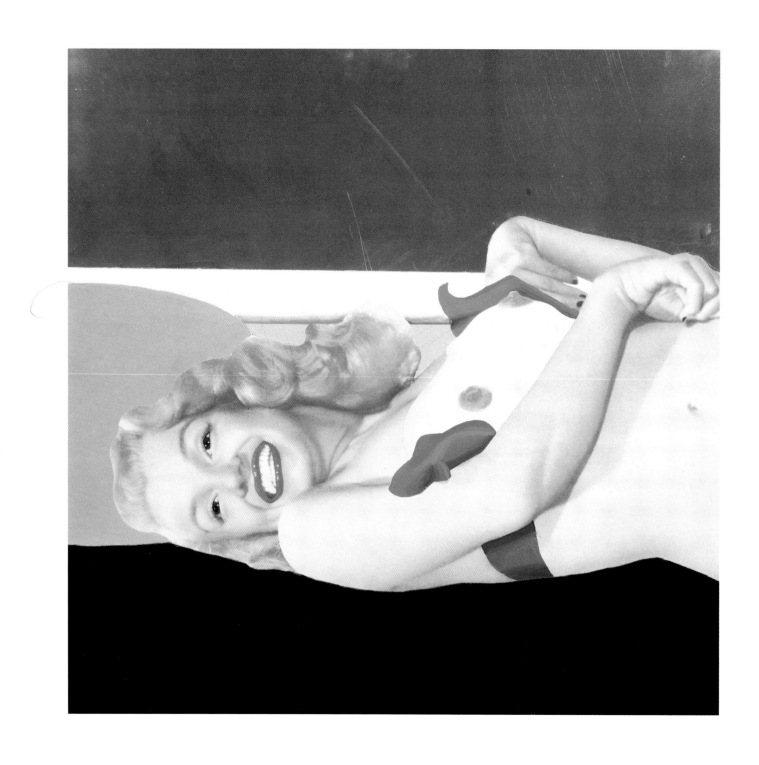

Tom Wesselmann (b. 1931). *Little Great American Nude #24*. 1965. Oil and collage on canvas, 24 x 24". Collection of Robert E. Abrams, New York.

Robert Indiana (b. 1928). *The Metamorphosis of Norma Jean Mortenson.* 1967. Acrylic on canvas, 102 x 102".
Collection of Robert L. B. Tobin, San Antonio.

especially an artist such as Hamilton, who often uses
a posteriori elements as collage or accommodation
for his resulting artwork.

Hamilton's choice of title speaks eloquently to his
assignment of authority. In the dense iconography of
images that are addressed to Monroe and that use
her image and portions thereof, there is only one
that declares that this version is the artist's and the
artist's alone. The possessive of the title shifts our
thinking to realize that Hamilton declares himself
the determining force of this image, not Monroe
and certainly not Hollywood or popular culture.
With a singular intensity among the artists identified with Pop art, Hamilton has repeatedly
declared a personal culling and cultivation from
popular culture, seldom with shared or expected values imputed to popular culture.
Hamilton is not the relatively passive
observer that Pop art propagated in such
instances as Roy Lichtenstein and Andy
Warhol. He seizes, thrashes, and
processes popular culture. He has
even taken hold of Monroe, declaring her "his."

In an analysis of Duchamp,
Thierry de Duve describes
the substance of his art
as being an act of nomination, not of creation.[3] Similarly,
Hamilton's art depends upon the
process of naming, which becomes
here an Old Testament–like model of
creation and possession, seizing by
notice and modulated interpretation. Of
course, it is this very act of nomination
that Hamilton here shares with Monroe,
allowing this work to be as fully his as it is
magnanimously hers. Who has ultimate dominion in this work, Hamilton or Monroe? What sets
Hamilton's image apart from myriad other representations of Monroe is the battle for sovereign-
ty, the image in contention between subject and
artist. That such Antaean struggle has subse-
quently become the basis for argumentation with
respect to mediation and the relative might of the
fine-arts image only corroborates its importance.
Further, the lack of a unified perspective is disori-
enting to the spectator, but also indicative of the
uncertainty of the image's assignment to artist or to
subject. Moreover, Hamilton offers his own enigma
of the image obliteration. Likening the "X" to a kiss
mark, Hamilton heightens the ambiguity of image
negation. The kiss by Monroe's operation would
inevitably be seduction or narcissism, yet it is also
rejection in this context. Strategies other than the
crossing-out also occur, notably in the large panel at

lower right, in which the figure is more or less cut out so that the bathing suit appears within a white silhouette, suggesting absence. Image alteration in other frames suggests that a curious pointillism used by Hamilton in *Bathers* and a de Kooning–esque imitation are also methods of withdrawing the image from viability, in these instances even augmenting the violating "X." Hamilton uses the visual techniques of image articulation and revocation throughout *My Marilyn* in order to secure his artistic authority. All of the images begin in photography, but Hamilton alone—surpassing Monroe—is capable of their transmogrification. The images that remain whole and select (the middle one marked "good") are the most photographically intact. Ultimately, the spectator's judgment is not the same as Monroe's, for Hamilton has fashioned most of the images into more painterly results. Hence, we are probably even disappointed in the image that Monroe selected for its lack of painterly inflection, now seemingly bland among its associated and highly evolved images. In this gesture, Hamilton has snatched Monroe's editorializing act away from her choice and taken it as his own judgment upon images. He offers an object lesson in the propaganda and propagation of images, rendering popular-culture selection a tedious choice among relative equals, all of which might benefit from art's greater involvement and the painterly intervention of the artist. Hamilton has chosen Monroe as his ostensible subject, but his real subject is popular culture and the media image. More than any other artist of the great obsessive and collective portrait of Monroe, he has practiced his deceits and waged his battle for power with Monroe in the very circumstances of what constitutes a contemporary image. But by commenting so directly on the editorial prerogatives demanded by Monroe, Hamilton takes us now into an image-determining process of popular culture and art in which we seldom trespass. He makes us aware of the power of the image. He makes us aware of Monroe's all-but-absolute power. But he also makes us aware of the limits of her power. In the end, she is not even "Marilyn," but the possessive and subjective of art and image, *My Marilyn*. After all of her mediation and manipulation, Monroe is nonetheless subject to further intervention. Long after the candle is extinguished, the smoke lingers.

Raymond Saunders (b. 1934). *Joseph Fitzpatrick Was Our Teacher.* 1991. Mixed media, 60 x 108".
Collection of Crocker Art Museum, Sacramento; gift of the Crocker Art Museum Association.

Elvis Presley's "Don't Be Cruel" is a song I've remembered well since the mid-fifties, when I first heard it as a young teenager. Counting on the likelihood that you know it too, my drawing suggests another meaning and requests that you forget for a moment the meaning and implications of Elvis' song and think of mine, futile as that might be.

William Wegman

William Wegman (b. 1943). *Elvis (Don't Be Cruel)*. 1982. Ink on paper, 11 x 14".
Courtesy of the artist.

James Strombotne (b. 1934). *Elvis and Alfalfa*. 1993. Acrylic on canvas, 36 x 36".
Courtesy of the artist and Sherry Frumkin Gallery, Santa Monica.

It is believed by many that a hundred years down the road Elvis will be a bona fide religion. I just can't wait.
Matthew Lawrence

Matthew Lawrence (b. 1965). *Elvis and the Sick Puppy*. 1989. Woodcut print on mulberry paper on canvas, 72 x 72".
Courtesy of the artist.

Roger Brown (b. 1941). *Don't Be Cruel.* 1989. Oil on canvas, 72 x 48". Greenville County Museum of Art, museum purchase with funds
donated by the Arthur and Holly Magill Foundation.

The painting Don't Be Cruel *was my response to the sighting phenomenon. Beloved public figures are often not allowed to simply rest in peace after their deaths.*
Roger Brown

I first became aware of Elvis during sixth-grade chorus, when one day the teacher asked us, "Who likes Elvis Presley?" and, since few were raising their hands, I decided to raise mine, the story of my life. I must have heard his early songs, though I think I was still listening to Big John and Sparkey and the Lone Ranger on the radio. I didn't really listen to music until the second year of high school, when I really began to hear Elvis, the Big Bopper, etc., at school dances and on radio KAFY from Bakersfield. These days I just collect the covers of the sleaziest tabloids which concern the King, wondering where they're getting all this great info and when will I run into him in a McDonald's. I must be firmly implanted into the myth. May I live as long!
David Gilhooly

David Gilhooly (b. 1943). *Frog Elvis: The Lounge Act.* 1993. White earthenware with commercial glaze, 15 x 13 x 13". Courtesy of the artist.

I chose the pseudonym of Rastas Foo in 1984 to create a second body of work with an identity and style being that of a folk artist or "outsider." To maximize the fictional character's marginalization and denied status within any minority, I made Rastas Foo the product of a union between African and Asian parentage.
The title A Foo of Sorts by Rastas Foo *refers to a kinship Rastas feels toward Elvis, due to Presley's preoccupation with both African-American rhythm and blues music and the Asian martial arts.*
Wayne Edson Bryan

Wayne Edson Bryan (b. 1957). *A Foo of Sorts by Rastas Foo.* 1990. Enamel on
wood diptych, 18 x 32". Courtesy of Gallery K, Washington, D.C.

John D. Baskerville

THE ACT OF SIGNIFYIN(G) IN POPULAR MUSIC: ELVIS PRESLEY AS A CULTURAL BRIDGE

It was more of a reading than a writing.
—Ishmael Reed

When the African was kidnapped and brought to this country to perform labor, he was forced to leave all material items behind. In most West African societies, these material objects were of no intrinsic value compared to the cultural customs and traditions that shaped the African's world view. Once he stepped foot on American soil, these would form the basis of African-American culture.[1]

Within the West African cultural matrix that accompanied these abducted immigrants were the trickster figures Esu-Elegbara (Nigeria) and Legba (Benin). Henry Louis Gates's *The Signifyin(g) Monkey: A Theory of African-American Literary Criticism* presents a theory of literary criticism based on the black vernacular expression called "signifyin(g)," traceable to West African tradition, which Gates applies to the double-voiced intertextual relations inherent in African-American literature. As a starting point, Gates looks to polytheistic West African cultures in which Esu-Elegbara, or Esu, serves as a liaison between the gods and man. "Esu is the guardian of the crossroads, master of style and stylus, the phallic god of generation and fecundity, master of that elusive, mystical barrier that separates the divine world from the profane."[2] Esu has several devices at his means to draw upon: "satire, parody, individuality, ambiguity, sexuality, chance, disruption, indeterminacy, open-endedness, betrayal" among others.[3] Esu is portrayed as "double voiced" (possessing two mouths) in Yoruba sculpture, since he is an interpreter of many languages and metaphors: the interpreter of texts. The myth of Esu was retained and adapted by African-American culture into the character of the "Signifyin(g) Monkey."

Besides being applied to African-American literature, Gates's methods can also be applied to African-American music. Anthropologist Clifford Geertz uses the metaphor of viewing culture as text as a way of interpreting cultural constructs.[4] George Marcus and Michael Fischer state that "social activities can be 'read' for their meaning by the observer just as written and spoken materials more conventionally are. What's more, not only the ethnographer reads symbols in action, but so do the observed—the actors in relation to one another."[5] Literary criticism in the past decade has developed an arsenal of theoretical approaches to interpret the construction of literary works: deconstruction, semiotics, hermeneutics, and reception theory, to name a few. These approaches can be used as tools to interpret cultural phenomena, if one employs the metaphor of culture as text. This metaphor of culture as text can be broken down into many of the areas that comprise culture: literature, art, and music.

To view music as text is fairly natural: like literature, music is constructed (composed) to achieve an aesthetic reaction. According to Bruce Tucker, musicologists have traditionally studied music, especially black music, from a "score-centered orbit," concentrating on the notes or formal relations:

The traditional musicologists who have trained the heavy artillery of European formalist analysis on black music, either sympathetically or maliciously, have generally achieved one of

My work comes from the southern narrative tradition. I thought it would be a good idea to substitute Elvis for Adam (Elvis being the first man of rock and roll). I see the image as the moment Elvis signed the management contract with Colonel Parker.
Francis Pavy

Francis Pavy (b. 1954). *Elvis and Eve.* 1993. Oil and enamel on copper, 26 x 24".
Courtesy of Arthur Roger Gallery, New Orleans.

 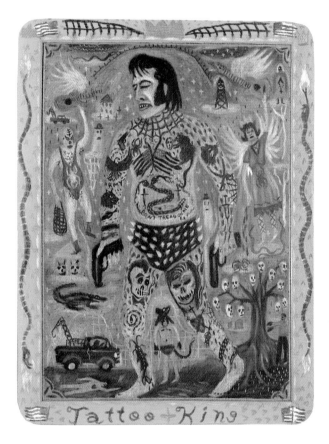

Tony Fitzpatrick (b. 1958). *Memphis Tattoo King*. 1988. Colored pencil and acrylic on slate, two parts, each 12½ x 9½".

Collection of George Felice, courtesy of Janet Fleisher Gallery, Philadelphia

two melancholy results: either transforming some black music into art music or concluding that all black music is inferior (which is finally the same thing) and leaving the cultural context—which is to say any conceivable significance—far behind. For the time being, then, black music inquiry will have to draw on the work of literary and cultural theorists, who have produced the most powerful explanatory models we have of black expressive practices.[6]

Coupling literary theory and literary criticism with formal relations of traditional musicology, we have an extensive epistemological framework on which to build.

Gates' study offers a good theoretical basis for the "reading" of African-American music. Drawing also on the work of Samuel A. Floyd, Jr., and Gary Tomlinson, it can be demonstrated that the act of "signifyin(g)" is present in the performances of Elvis Presley, largely because of his close contact with African-American culture.

The Signifyin(g) Monkey is a quasi-mythic African-American trickster figure of and from the vernacular tradition of folktales. According to Gates, the Monkey speaks in an open-ended figurative language that is "open to (mis)interpretation."[7] He continues:

Signifyin(g) is black double-voicedness; because it always entails formal revision and an intertextual relation, and because of Esu's double-voiced representation in art, I find it an ideal metaphor for black literary criticism, for the formal manner in which texts seem concerned to address their antecedents.[8]

The Monkey "signifies" on those animate and inanimate objects around him. Present in the act of signifyin(g) are standard literary tropes, such as "metaphor, metonymy, synecdoche and irony . . . also hyperbole, litotes, and metalepsis," as well as devices of black rhetorical discourse, such as "marking, loud-talking, testifying, calling (of one's name), sounding, rapping, playing the dozens, and so on."[9] Through their figurative and implicative language, tales of the Signifyin(g) Monkey turn power relationships on their heads. The weak can disable the strong through a verbal assault of metaphor and misdirection. Being a combination of the vernacular and the formal, literature of African-American and Caribbean writers constitutes a double-voiced tradition in which texts signify upon their antecedents. The Signifyin(g) Monkey serves as interpreter between the vernacular and formal worlds of literature, in the same way as Esu acted as liaison between the gods and man.

Gates emphasizes that the act of signifyin(g), due to its intertextuality, is a mediating strategy assuming a position between or among texts or cultural traditions that gives it, in Gary Tomlinson's words, a "dialogical essence":

[It] is signaled in the concept of vernacular theory. Vernacular thought emphasizes its own boundaries, its own range of authority and territorial claims, in counterpoint with other theoretical domains. Because of this, vernacularism is a mode of thought that attempts, in contrast to transcendentalism, universalism, and essentialism, to theorize the space between itself and others—to keep sight, so to speak, of other modes of thought around it by keeping them above its horizon. In the case of Gates' theory of black expressive culture, Signification represents, on the most general plane, the linguistic mediation between black vernacular(s) and the discourse(s) of white hegemonic culture.[10]

In essence, signifyin(g) works as a complex figure rooted in the conflation of traditional, often rough, denigrating, profane, yet intellectually challenging wordplay known as "playing the dozens," a teenage rite of passage for black males of the Jim Crow South[11]—with the correspondingly parodic, ambiguous, double-voiced language attributed to the trickster Esu of Yoruba culture. Both worlds overlap in the Signifyin(g) Monkey, and the two linguistic traditions antecede, according to Gates, the figurative, satirical, disparaging, bonding, mocking, often punning vernacular posture and one-upmanship known as signifyin(g)—the "trope of tropes" that is both insult and tribute.[12] In the same way that signifyin(g) serves as Gates's metaphor for literary criticism, it is metaphorically apt in the study of Elvis Presley.

In his performances, Presley attempted to establish a dialogue between black and white popular music through the use of intertextuality, drawing from both traditions. According to Samuel Floyd, black music mediates between black vernacular oral culture and European music. Floyd believes that musical genres signify on other musical genres as "a way of demonstrating respect for, goading, or poking fun at a musical style, process, or practice through parody, pastiche, implication, indirection, humor, tone- or word-play, the illusion of speech or narration, and other troping mechanisms."[13]

Presley was heavily influenced, directly and indirectly, by African-American culture. Southern culture, particularly southern white vernacular music, contains many Africanisms, but this aspect of southern history until recently has been seldom addressed. It is important to examine the existence of this African-American influence on the South in order to demonstrate the indirect influence on Presley's life and music, equipping him to serve as a musical and cultural bridge.

* * *

Southern whites cannot walk, talk, sing, conceive of laws or justice, think of sex, love, the family or freedom without responding to the presence of the Negroes.
—Ralph Ellison

Acculturation is a two-way process: one takes elements from the dominant culture, while at the same time giving something back. Of Africans and Europeans in the New World, Nathan Irvin Higgins states, "Perhaps the most affecting experience in their transformation was in adapting to each other."[14] Yet few books or articles have been written concerning African contributions to American society. Cultural anthropologist Melville J. Herskovits, who was at the forefront of this discourse in the first half of the century, has examined some of the Africanisms present in American society, particularly those pertaining to language and music.[15] Historian C.

Vann Woodward, in a 1969 article attempting to convince more whites to enter the field of black studies, stated that some whites contain more Africanisms than some blacks.[16]

Through close daily contact with enslaved and free blacks, whites gradually began to adopt Africanisms in their culture. Primary in this cultural exchange was the fact that many white upper-class children were raised by black women during the antebellum period. The acculturation of white children, through contact with their black caretakers, became so alarming that the antebellum clergy warned the slaveholders to be cautious of the influence slaves had on their children. It was feared that these influences would remain with the children for the rest of their lives.[17]

Many white children absorbed African cultural elements until southern white culture eventually became somewhat African in nature. Nowhere can this influence be seen more than in the area of music. This is why Alice Walker's narrator, Gracie Mae Still, in the short story "Nineteen Fifty-Five," says, "I don't know why I called him Son. Well, one way or another they're all our sons."[18] Gracie Mae, representative of Willie Mae "Big Mama" Thornton, is speaking of the white male protagonist Traynor, representative of Elvis Presley, who has recorded one of her songs. Not only does Gracie Mae represent Thornton, she also represents all of the black female singers who influenced Elvis ever since the early stages of rock and roll.

African-American music, and the influence of African music and culture on it, forms the basis of most, if not all, American music. So far, little scholarship has been devoted to the African origins of white American folk music, yet there is clear evidence to suggest that white Appalachian and early country music have several Africanisms present. The banjo, an African instrument, has become so prevalent among white folk and country musicians that many have mistaken its origins as European. Yet even the playing style of the instrument can be traced back to West Africa:

Banjos are often struck on the head while being played, a technique characteristic of Senegambian music. Improvisation and the solo-chorus response style of singing—both so characteristic of Africa—are notable features of bluegrass music. Syncopation is built into American traditional music, at least in the South, in a way alien to British music of the eighteenth century.[19]

Yodeling is another common performance technique, prevalent in white folk and country music, which can also be traced to African origins. Yodeling occurs in the music of many African regions and in the field hollers of African-American rural life. Jimmie Rodgers, who is considered by some to be the father of country music, incorporated yodeling in his singing

William Eggleston (b. 1939). *Untitled (Gold Piano)*. 1983. Dye transfer print, 24 x 20".
Collection of The Chase Manhattan Bank, N.A.

Someone ordered a custom-designed guitar with Marilyn Monroe's face painted on it. The order was later declined or a duplicate was made, because I found the "Marilyn guitar" at a musical instrument store on 48th Street in New York. Imagine Elvis hugging Marilyn, the great seductress; serenading her, singing a lullaby to her.
Haim Steinbach

Haim Steinbach (b. 1944). *Untitled (breast mugs, Marilyn guitar) I–1.* 1990.
Plastic laminated wood shelf with objects, 74½ x 54¼ x 29". Courtesy of Sonnabend Gallery and Jay Gorney Modern Art, New York.

style. Eventually it would evolve into the "break" in many country singers voices. "Rodgers grew up where blacks were in the majority, and his singing shows profound black influences in other respects as well as his yodeling."[20]

White secular music was not the only music affected; white sacred music would also adopt many Africanisms. The religious movement known as the Second Awakening, which flourished in America from 1780 to 1830, was a revival movement primarily drawing the working class of all Protestant faiths, both black and white. Eileen Southern has described the format of these meetings:

A continuous religious service spread out over several days, often an entire week. Religious services took place in a forest or woods [similar to the "invisible" church meetings established by slaves], the members of the huge temporary congregations worshiping in large tents and living in small tents.[21]

By 1818 black churches began to establish their own camp meetings, which continued to draw thousands of worshipers, both black and white. In these black-run camp meetings, musical performance practices evolved in a different direction from their white counterparts. While in the white-run meetings the music primarily consisted of the religious hymns of Isaac Watts, performed as written, in the black-run meetings, the congregations adapted the Watts hymns to meet their own needs as well as composing new songs:

First, the blacks were holding songfests away from proper supervision, and this was undesirable in the eyes of the [white] church fathers. They were singing songs of their own composing, which was even worse in the eyes of the officials. The texts of the composed songs were not lyric poems in the hallowed tradition of Watts, but a stringing together of isolated lines from prayers, the Scriptures, and orthodox hymns, the whole made longer by the addition of choruses or the injecting of refrains between verses. Finally, for their composed religious songs the blacks used tunes that were dangerously near to being dance tunes in the style of slave jubilee melodies. . . . [F]rom such practices emerged a new kind of religious song that became the distinctive badge of the camp-meeting movement.[22]

These newly composed songs would incorporate many of the Africanisms of black secular music—call and response, improvisation, and an emotional delivery, to name a few. Whites would eventually adopt these spiritual songs and performance techniques and incorporate them into their religious services.

In the 1850s another religious movement, the Protestant City Revival movement, would cause yet another major shift in religious music practices. The music that developed was called "gospel." Whereas the camp meetings and the spiritual songs were a rural phenomenon, this new movement took place in the urban setting:

in huge temporary tents erected for revival meetings by touring evangelists. . . . The gospel hymnwriters incorporated the traditions of the early nineteenth-century camp-meeting songs in their hymns, using stanza-chorus forms and hymns with refrains; they also borrowed forms and melodies from popular songs . . . just as their predecessors had borrowed folksongs and popular tunes for religious songs many decades earlier.[23]

As Southern implies, these gospel hymns originated with the signifyin(g) musical practices of African-Americans during the Second Awakening.[24]

Through close proximity and interaction in the South, blacks and whites began to adopt cultural traits from each other, establishing a distinct southern culture. The music of a white performer/songwriter from this region who was never formally exposed to black music would naturally contain an African-American flavor, since white music signifies on black music through cultural osmosis. If this same white performer/songwriter were exposed directly to black music—as in the case of Elvis Presley—through close listening and interaction with black musicians, his music is liable to contain high concentrations of Africanisms, including the act of signifyin(g).

In *The Sound of the City: The Rise of Rock and Roll* (1983), Charlie Gillett, using a model developed by sociologist Talcott Parsons regarding the process by which a minority group achieves social acceptance, applies it to black music during the postwar period in America. The first stage of the process is *exclusion*, "when the minority group as a whole is denied the privileges enjoyed by the rest of society."[25] Blues and rhythm and blues were excluded from the mainstream hit parades, radio airplay, and major record labels due to racism and the belief that the musical content and lyrics were too close to the black musical tradition for the white audience to understand.

The second stage of the process is *assimilation*, "when these privileges are granted to favored members of the minority group but continue to be withheld from the rest."[26] Those accepted few are included on the condition, to paraphrase Gillett, that they break all cultural ties with the minority group's culture and adopt the standards of mainstream society. Gillett believes there were two types of assimilation operating at the time: first, "to adopt black singers who adopted styles that were specifically developed for the white audience (and so had little relation to styles popular with the black audience)" and second, "to take a song or style from the black culture and reproduce it using a white singer."[27]

Although blacks themselves have not yet reached the final stage, inclusion, it will be achieved "when the entire minority group is granted access to everything in society, without having to yield its distinctive characteristics. . . . The established society [must modify] its relationship with the minority group, adjusting its attitudes and mobilizing its institutions to accommodate the group."[28] While black artists in the 1950s were opening the door for other blacks to pass through by showing the music industry that black music could be profitable, white artists, with Elvis Presley at the vanguard, were exposing a growing mass audi-

ence to songs and performing styles that had once been viewed as alien. Unconsciously or consciously, Presley would serve as a bridge between black music culture and the white mainstream.

Presley differed from typical cover artists because of his immersion in southern culture and consequent connections with black culture. He differed even more because of his genuine love of black music. On Elvis' tastes, it has been noted that "probably the only kinds of music he didn't care for were jazz and opera."[29] Presley especially had a love for black gospel music, which was nurtured in his youth.

Elvis grew up in Tupelo, Mississippi, on the edge of a black section of town known as "Shakerag," where he was exposed to black gospel blues. Former Mississippi radio announcer Ernest Bowen has noted that young white boys interested in music often sat in on and listened to Sanctified Church services. In her book *Elvis and Gladys*, Elaine Dundy writes of Elvis listening to the music in these services.[30] Elvis continued to listen to black gospel music throughout his life:

[He owned] a huge collection of black gospel and jubilee records. Some were 78's dating from as far back as the twenties. Never a gospel buff myself, I unfortunately cannot recall the titles or the artists who sang on the records Elvis cherished. But there was one gospel singer Elvis often spoke of and admired, a black reverend named Jimmy Jones. . . . Elvis had his records and was fascinated as much by his personality and legend as by his voice.[31]

Through his listening, Presley was exposed to several gospel singers as well as to the various black religious singing styles, and their significant common denominator was the pattern of signifyin(g): "Gospel music concentrated more on the interplay between voices," notes Gillett, "which were often deliberately coarsened to stress the emotional conviction of the singers."[32]

Besides his exposure to black gospel blues, Presley, with his mother, attended white folk churches (Assembly of God) throughout his youth, and he performed in the church at age two. The influences of the black and white churches would have a lasting effect on Presley's singing style. Christianity was of fundamental importance in Elvis' life and gospel music was a primary element in his singing.

Presley succeeded in combining white gospel hymns with a black gospel-blues singing style. Both traditions are evident in Presley's performance of "Joshua Fit the Battle" (1960) where he emulates the singing style of Mahalia Jackson. Their signifyin(g) interrelationship becomes clear when Jackson's performance of "Walk in Jerusalem" is juxtaposed with Presley's performance. Both singers use their vocal dexterity (making leaps of an octave in pitch) to emphasize par-

Laurens Tan (b. 1950). . . . *well, the image is one thing* . . . . 1992–94.
Video installation. Courtesy of the artist.

Keith Haring (1958–1990). *Untitled*. 1981. Sumi ink on printed poster, 38½ x 26¾".
The Estate of Keith Haring.

Left: Keith Haring (1958–1990). *Untitled*. 1981. Sumi ink and metallic ink on printed poster, 38½ x 26¾". The Estate of Keith Haring.
Right: Keith Haring (1958–1990). *Untitled*. 1981. Sumi ink, marker ink, and metallic marker on printed poster, 38½ x 26¾". The Estate of Keith Haring.

ticular pas-
sages and words within the chorus and some of the verses. Presley also
adopts Jackson's dark, rich timbre, which comes to
the forefront in the lower vocal range, where both achieve
a percussive effect by accenting the hard consonants of the
words and giving the music a syncopated rhythmic feel. Presley's
seemingly improvisational performance of these black gospel singing
techniques operates against the rhythmically straight, harmonic background vocals of a white gospel quartet, the Jordanaires.
Presley's love of the black gospel sound was evident in his performances of
secular music. He achieved this sound through the use of the group "The Sweet
Inspirations" as backup vocalists. The black community had already experienced the
combination of the sacred with the secular in their music, but this was a
foreign concept to most in the white mainstream.[33] Although many
critics dismiss Presley's Las Vegas years, the style of his performances there were reminiscent of the revival meetings during
the Protestant City Revival movement.
One of Presley's performances of "See See Rider" (1970, Las
Vegas) contains many of the elements of a gospel revival.
The most noticeable is the call and response occurring
between Presley, the Sweet Inspirations, and the instrumentalists. Presley sings the melody during the chorus (the call)
and is backed by the repeated refrains of "Yeah, Yeah, Yeah"
and "See See Rider." The Sweet Inspirations resemble a
choir during the "See See Rider" refrains while also assuming the role of congregation through the singing of the
"Yeah, Yeah, Yeah." A three-way call and response is
achieved by the exchanges between the instrumentalists
and the Sweet Inspirations: the vocalists respond to Presley
and the instrumentalists respond to the vocalists.
As an act of signifyin(g), Presley's Las Vegas rendition of
"See See Rider" contains many of the elements of LaVern
Baker's performance of the song (1960), but retains its own
identity. Both performances emphasize call and response
as well as a high emotional level, but Presley's version has
more drive due to the larger ensemble and the walking line
in the bass. Presley also makes use of the kinds of sudden
changes in dynamics that give his singing a preaching
sound.
Presley was also exposed to black secular music through
radio, records, and live performances. He paid close attention
to the performances of black artists and incorporated their techniques into his performances—hence, signifyin(g). By some
accounts, Elvis' stage act suggested more than the double-voiced mediative
discourse that Gates examines. By Dundy's account, Elvis' performing style was
an eclectic signifyin(g) composite, in which black rhythm and blues, white
country music, black and white gospel rock, and other styles, like that of
Dean Martin, were synthesized. His body movements signified on Johnnie
Ray, with the flailing arms and gyrating of Bo Diddley and the stomp-
ing of Little Richard.[34]
Presley had a passion for soul singing. Besides Jackie Wilson,
whom Presley idolized, James Brown had a prolonged
impact on Presley's music. Presley said of him, "They
all copy him, but no one's got the soul of
James Brown."[35] The two shared a
mutual respect and cultivated
a friendship.

In his auto-
biography Brown speaks of it:

At a big party he threw in the Hyatt Continental,
I think, when it got late, we threw everybody out of the
room, and Elvis and I sang gospel together. . . . That's how
we communicated—by singing jubilee, the real upbeat kind of
gospel. He told me he wanted to use my band to record. He said he
wanted horns and things behind him, but he wanted them strong.
When he first started he was copying B. B. [King] and them, but finally
they didn't have enough fire for him. That's when he really got into his own
thing. Elvis was great.[36]

Presley's performance of "Polk Salad Annie" (1970) signifies on the funk
style of James Brown. Though Presley's rendition is close to the
original by Tony Joe White (1969), the funk groove established by
the instrumentalists is reminiscent of the JB's, Brown's instru-
mental ensemble. Presley's band takes White's arrangement
and gives it more drive by foregrounding the syncopated bass
line. The horn section and the Sweet Inspirations add fills by
riffing and they serve as a response to Elvis' signifyin(g) call.
Another performance in which Presley signifies on Brown, as
well as himself, is a Madison Square Garden performance of
"Hound Dog" (1972). Once again, Presley is backed with a
funk groove that rewrites his 1956 performance as a parody of
it. The slow groove allows Presley to "rap" the lyrics instead
of singing them, giving the performance a playful quality.
In his career, Presley did not forget his country roots; much
of his secular music includes strong Chet Atkins–like guitar
playing. To be sure, Presley signified on white musical tradition—Hank Williams, Jimmie Rodgers, Mario Lanza—as
much as on the characteristics of black music. This multicultural interaction of voices and traditions gives Presley's
music the quality of "stir-fry"—several different styles mixed
together while retaining their essence.
Some have accused Presley of stealing fame and fortune
from the black artists whose songs he recorded. James
Brown discusses this issue: "Cats complain all the time about
white people learning music from blacks. It's true we've kind
of had a monopoly on certain kinds of music, but everybody's
entitled to it. They shouldn't steal it, but they're entitled to learn
it and play it. No sense in keeping all the drive on one side,
because if you're teaching people, you're teaching people."[37]
Elvis Presley's performances subverted, like the tales of the
Signifyin(g) Monkey, some of the traditional power relationships of white and
black, sacred and secular postwar musical cultures. In doing so, he accomplished an extraordinary educational feat. Just as Esu moved between the
spiritual and human worlds, Presley traveled between black and white cultures during a time when most whites in American society, artists or
otherwise, were content to remain within the confines of their own
cultures. This willingness to serve as a cultural bridge is what
makes Elvis Presley a unique figure in popular music.
Through listening to Elvis Presley and watching him perform, white society began to learn, in the lazy,
quasi-conscious way of the 1950s and early
1960s, that African-American culture had something impor-
tant to offer.

Sally Davies (b. 1956). *Del Rey*. 1987. Oil on canvas, 24 x 18".
Courtesy of the artist.

Howard Finster (b. 1916). *Elvis For His Country (#2077)*. 1981. Enamel and marker on wood, 15½ x 19½". Collection of Dr. and Mrs. William M. Colaiace, Providence; courtesy of Phyllis Kind Gallery, Chicago/New York.

64/150

R. Lindner

Richard Lindner (1901–1978). *Marilyn Was Here*. 1976. One of 17 lithographs, Plexiglas portfolio, 17½ x 13⅛".
Collection of Colette and Achim Moeller, New York.

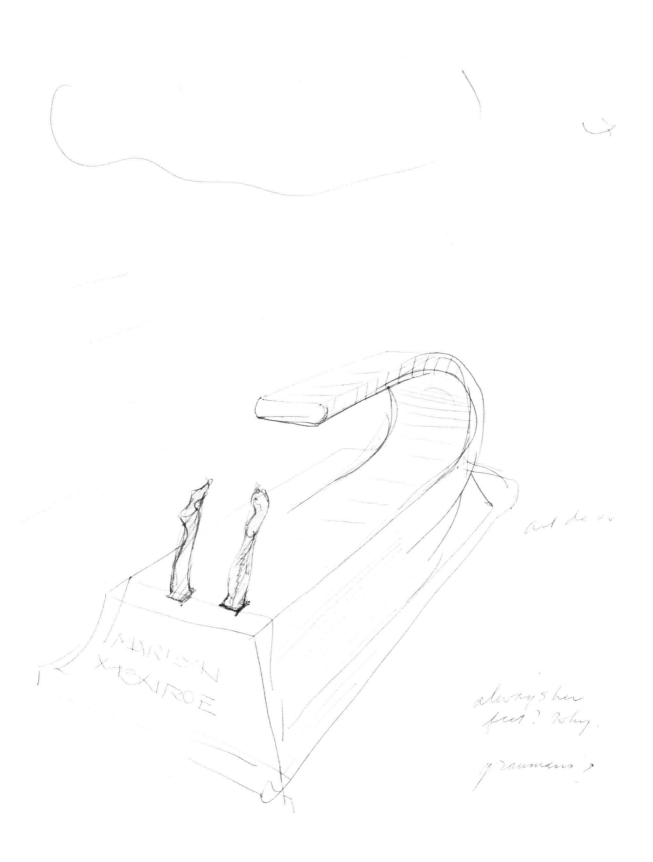

Claes Oldenburg (b. 1929). *Notebook Page: Tomb Design for Marilyn Monroe.* 1960s. Ball-point pen and colored pencil, 11 x 8½".
Collection of Claes Oldenburg and Coosje van Bruggen, New York.

The pixels remind me that Elvis, and all things, consist of temporary collections of atomic and subatomic particles, waves, and vibration. Elvis happened to be one of those most unique collections passing through in his time. I always loved the electrical Frankenstein effect of this accidental print. It's as if he is so charged up that strings of energy are coming out of him. I also like the tragic look of his face and inference of blood in the reds. The prisoner of the human form dancing to the ecstasy and the horrors of fate and fame. Although I have always lived in Memphis, I never saw Elvis. My father went to Humes High School at the same time Elvis did, and he said, "He always dressed funny, and he wore pants with piping down the sides, greaser style." My mom remembers him at an impromptu performance behind a shopping center, playing for five or six passersby.
Roy Tamboli

Roy Tamboli (b. 1951). *Elvis.* 1993. Cibachrome photograph of computer-altered silkscreen, 45 x 33".
Courtesy of the artist.

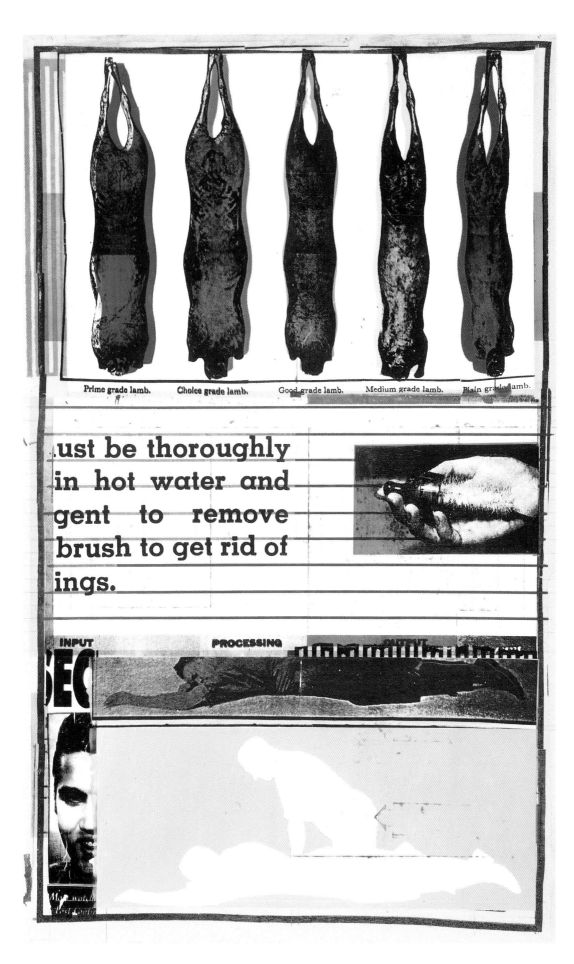

Steven Dunning (b. 1957). *Untitled*. 1991. Acrylic on canvas, 51¾ x 32".

Courtesy of the artist.

THE GOD AND GODDESS OF THE WRITTEN WORD

Lucinda Ebersole

The era that we live in is an age of postmodernism. One of the most startling differences between this current era and the not-so-distant modernist period is the proliferation of media. In the first decades of the century, when Margaret Anderson braved the cold winds of Chicago and laid out the copy for her influential magazine, the *Little Review,* and Nancy Cunard struggled in Paris at her Hours Press to bring to the world the words of black writers, neither could have imagined the growth of the publishing industry nor the ease with which printed text can now be delivered on a page. The computer has revolutionized the way that text is gathered, retrieved, and printed. Computers have evolved from warehouse-sized contraptions for doing mathematical equations to the small plastic boxes found in so many homes and offices.

At the same time that the printed word has been transformed, the visual media have proliferated. Television captures the visual image and projects it into our living rooms and bedrooms. Movies fill the big screens in theaters. Video combines them by putting movies on television screens. Our way of telling stories has gone through a revolution. Coupling the computer and visual image provides a way to create images that exist only in the imagination. Compare *The Creature from the Black Lagoon* with *Jurassic Park.* Movie-making has been transformed.

The more society is inundated with visual images, the more it wants to see them—and see them in a different way. The slow black-and-white camera of "Perry Mason" has given way to the florid color and quick cuts of "Miami Vice."

How has the proliferation of the visual affected today's writers? In the same way that society and culture have always affected the writers of a particular generation. Writers view the society around them and translate it to the page. In the postmodern era, it is not surprising that the work of writers reflects the explosion of the visual, including its compelling iconography. A major reflection of this process is the emergence in literature of Elvis Presley and Marilyn Monroe.

In the past ten years there has been a steady stream of stories, novels, plays, and films about Elvis and Marilyn—as if they are on their way to becoming a genre unto themselves—with entire sections of bookstores devoted to their titles: Civil War, Gardening, Elvis & Marilyn. Why has this happened? What has made two individuals whose primary window of fame existed in the 1950s become literary legends of the 1990s?

Finding answers to these questions is as easy as opening one's eyes and looking, or as complicated as understanding the effects of visual images on anyone. Elvis and Marilyn are everywhere. We see them in the movies they made, in movies about them, on coffee mugs, on postcards, on billboards, on clothing, in newspapers and magazines, in life-size cutouts, and in dolls fashioned in their image. The possibilities seem inexhaustible. Is the interminable proliferation of their images enough to spawn further repetition, or does something else occur? Are Elvis and Marilyn merely what we see, or have their images been transformed into something more?

With the attention paid to the images of Elvis and Marilyn, there is clearly something more at work than familiarity. What today has emerged from their image is what concerns us most, beyond the details of two well-known lives that are easily compressed into a few paragraphs.

Elvis Presley was born into crushing poverty in the South. His twin brother died. His mother bought him a guitar when he was young and he played for her. His life appeared to be headed nowhere. Though his music seemed to be uninspired, he possessed a quality that would lift him from his obscurity and make him a star. The good ol' boy from Tupelo, Mississippi, had a vocal quality that mimicked the sound of many black performers of the day, performers who could not be played on the radio because they were black. Elvis covered their songs, went on to make movies, married, divorced, and finally watched his career fade. He became a Las Vegas lounge singer in sequined jumpsuits who maintained a loyal following of mostly female fans.

Marilyn Monroe was born Norma Jeane Baker, an illegitimate child who suffered with her own poverty. As a child in southern California, she saw the world as a movie stage. Married at sixteen, she was determined

to be a star, even if it meant taking off
her clothes to do it. On the road to stardom she became
a blond and she became Marilyn Monroe. She did indeed make it to
the movies and though her professional career took off, her personal life
floundered. She seemed to have as many husbands as movies. She married a
baseball player and a playwright and was rumored to have fallen for a president. She
died of a drug overdose at thirty-six.
Neither lived a life of illumination nor of any particular valor that should catapult them to
the ranks of the revered. What they share is a unique time in history, a time where the cultural paradigm was shifting. Both were products of the 1950s, the last great bastion of tradi-
tionalism. The decade of the 1960s saw a tremendous change in the culture. There was a push
for equal rights for blacks and women, conflict over the war in Vietnam, riots in the streets, a
sexual revolution, a theological notion that God was dead.

Elvis Presley and Marilyn Monroe were the harbingers of the coming age
who lived before their time. They pushed the edges of what was traditional, and when that tradition broke apart, they were remembered
as pioneers. Our memory of them comes not so much from their
lives as from their transformation into cultural icons, which are
more powerful than either individual. The facts of their biogra-
phies are no longer of any concern to us; it is their afterlife
with which we are obsessed.

The Greek *eikon* is defined as an image or pictorial representation. The sheer volume of images of Elvis and Marilyn would
certainly classify them as icons. Icon can also be defined as an
object of uncritical devotion—an idol. Both have received their share
of a type of devotion from fans that borders on something more. The religious meaning
of the word "icon" suggests that the images of Elvis and Marilyn have transcended
the representational and moved to the sacred.
As with any culture, regardless of how secular ours might appear to have
become, we look for those stories and histories that hold society
together. We need a mythology, something bigger than we are.
A myth, generally defined as a traditional story of ostensibly historical events that can explain practice or belief, can also be a parable or an alle-
gory. The stories of Elvis and Marilyn are ostensibly historical, but do they serve
a larger purpose as the myths of a generation? Can Elvis and Marilyn be viewed as the
Zeus and Aphrodite of the postmodern era?
If so, then it follows that they should have a mythology. Today's writers have taken up the
challenge of creating a mythology that rivals the visual image. There is an irony in
a task that is in and of itself a fitting parable of the postmodern age. In
our traditional myth-making process, the word came first. Homer,
Aeschylus, and Euripides told the stories of the gods, and the sculp-
tors Phidias, Praxiteles, and Lysippus provided the visual images. In
postmodern mythology the tables are turned. For the postmodern
myth-maker, the visual image precedes the story. The overwhelm-
ing and repetitive force of the visual image bombarding television
picture tubes, movie screens, and popular advertising has given
rise to a mythology that springs from the image itself. In the
beginning is the visual image, and from the visual, myths arise.
If Elvis and Marilyn are popular icons, and if they now are gar-
nering a mythology that tells their stories while explaining our
belief, then it stands to reason that they are indeed the postmodern god and goddess of the age.

ELVIS AS ZEUS

The postmodern myth of Elvis presents us with a god. He is a
misunderstood but benevolent creature. He attracts disciples who
believe he can do no wrong, imitators who replicate his gesture and
dress, followers who make pilgrimages to the Mecca that is

Kathy Yancey (b. 1951). *Idol Worship Is a Bed of Roses.* 1987. Watercolor and gouache with collage, 23 x 22".
Collection of Richard and Barbara Dobkin.

Kathy Yancey (b. 1951). *Worshipping Venus From Afar.* 1992. Gouache and collage on board, 30½ x 29½".
Collection of John C. Yancey, Atlanta.

Nancy Burson (b. 1948). *Baby Elvis.* 1989–90. Photolithograph on silk, 38¾ x 30½".
Courtesy of Jayne H. Baum Gallery, New York.

Nancy Burson (b. 1948). *Baby Marilyn.* 1989–90. Photolithograph on silk, 38¾ x 30½".
Courtesy of Jayne H. Baum Gallery, New York.

Graceland. He offers a path to righteousness, a cure for those who are sick, and according to many, a transcendence of death. He exists in the present. His life offers the elements from which the gods of mythology are made.

Writers today have resurrected Elvis. He came into the world in a miraculous fashion. The odds were against him, but he survived the birth. A twin brother did not. Poet and rocker Nick Cave writes, "The King is born in Tupelo."[1] Elvis walked the earth among us and we watched as he descended into hell— a hell filled with drugs and sequined jumpsuits. Once he was dead, however, Elvis became the myth. In a novel by Laura Kalpakian, the extent of Elvis' power after death becomes evident:

Nailed up across the two front porch windows there was an American flag and a Confederate flag and below them a picnic table covered with a sheet, bleached, and starched, and ironed. The table reverently displayed a Gideon Bible at either end. A wreath of plastic daisies lay before a poster-sized picture of the mature Elvis wearing a white spangled bodysuit with a flaring cape. . . . Also on the white-clad table, smaller pictures of the young Elvis sat, some cut from newspapers, all in cheap metal frames, and at either end a vase of tall gladiolas in clear, unyellowed water. More red glads were tucked in the flag holder on the porch posts above yet another picture, Elvis in a Hawaiian lei. Nailed to a trellis, a huge hand-lettered sign read:

"Sacred to the Memory of This Prince Among Men
Elvis Aaron Presley

Long Live the King
His Truth Goes Marching On"[2]

Kalpakian's main character, Joyce, is a mother on welfare trying to raise her two daughters, Cillia and Lisa-Marie. Her husband left Joyce on the very day that Elvis died. Far from being downtrodden by her situation, Joyce perpetuates the indomitable spirit of a world animated by the Elvis mythos. When asked by her social worker, Emily, what she wants to do with her life, Joyce replies:

"I'd like to carry on Elvis' work. . ."
"You want to be a rock-and-roll star?"
"That wasn't his work. That was his job."[3]

Joyce, as Elvis had before her, continued to take care of business. For some writers, Elvis has achieved the ultimate in resurrection. It is both metaphorical and physical. And as only Elvis could, he rose from a faked death and landed in the most unlikely of places. In her story "Elvis, Axl and Me," Janice Eidus tells of her encounter with Elvis:

Elvis was the only other customer besides me. He was sitting at the next table. I could tell it was him right away, even though he was dressed up as a Hasidic Jew. He was wearing a yarmulke on top of his head, and a lopsided, shiny black wig with long payes on the sides that drooped past his chin, a fake looking beard to his collarbone, and a shapeless black coat, which didn't hide his paunch, even sitting down. His skin was as white as flour, and his eyes looked glazed, as though he spent far too much time indoors.[4]

The resurrected Elvis, whether dead or alive, turns up in the most amazing situations. Elvis is indeed everywhere.

While some writers see a traditional divinity in the mythology of Elvis, others view this sort of fascination as a cult. Michael Wilkerson's short story "The Elvis Cults" gives us a futurist view of a group of Elvis followers who have taken over a city in Indiana. Everyone looks like Elvis, and if they don't there is always surgery. Wilkerson writes:

Elvism had become the second largest religion in America. There was a picture of Bloomington's mayor, who looked like Him. The cults were centered in the south and midwest; they ranged from the quiet, meditative "singalikes" of Wisconsin and Minnesota to the more severe, cloistered "lookalikes" of Elvisville, portions of Illinois, and the Deep South. All Elvists were required to visit Memphis once during their lifetimes. Each day they turned toward that city and sang His lyrics.[5]

Every god needs followers, and Elvis is no exception. When Rafael Alvarez brings Elvis back in "The Annunciation," he does so in a more classically Christian sense; he has Elvis impregnate a virgin:

. . . the restless spirit of Elvis Presley returned to Earth through the ripe womb of a 15-year-old Jewish virgin named Ruthie as the girl floated helplessly over the rooftops of Baltimore. . . . This good news was heralded throughout the cosmos but passed unnoticed on the blue planet where it was rendered; a fantastic event absent from Ruthie's long list of plans.[6]

It might seem easy to look at the writings about Elvis and believe them to be just stories. One could argue that the idea of imposing mythology on a deceased rock-and-roll singer is silly, or that there is no particular significance to the often overt use of religious metaphor in these writings. Many might scoff at the power of the visual image of Elvis seen over and over to generate anything more than mere fiction. At least one editorial writer has speculated:

I have turned to these two legendary figures in my creations. My formative years in the Soviet Union were spent under the bright stars of these two demigods. "Stalin—The Father of All Races," "Stalin is the Wings of Our Youth," "Stalin Inspires Us for Heroic Feats in Work and Battle"—these songs blared from all public loudspeakers after the war and in the early 1950s. Stalin was everything—air, water, teacher, father generalissimos, etc. Marilyn Monroe became the spirit of America and success, the realization of the American Dream and an example for countless imitators.
Leonid Sokov

Leonid Sokov (b. 1941). *Marilyn and Stalin.* 1990. Oil on metal, 28½ x 21".
Collection of Mina Litinsky, Sloane Gallery of Art, Denver.

Malcah Zeldis (b. 1931). *Andy and Marilyn.* 1974. Oil on board, 48 x 36".
Courtesy of the artist.

Andrew Logan (b. 1945). *Marilyn [Glamour]–Lenin [Monumental].* 1991. Resin, glass, and wood,
Marilyn 62 x 44", *Lenin* 56 x 45". Courtesy of the artist.

. . . the possibility that a century hence the followers of Elvis Presley will constitute a religion. . . . The signs are there: a million devoted followers worldwide, torchlight rituals with an eternal flame at Graceland on the anniversary of Elvis's death, a consistent minority of Americans who tell pollsters that Elvis may still be alive and people who report visions of Elvis, comforting messages from Elvis and a sense of his nearness to them in times of trouble.[7]

MARILYN AS APHRODITE

Marilyn Monroe's is a different mythology. In looking at Marilyn, we can see the parallels of fanatical worship, but its focus and direction differ from that of Elvis. She illuminates the way that society has consistently viewed specific gender roles. She is always the goddess; as such, she is an object. Her myth portrays the way women are viewed in the postmodern age.

Marilyn Monroe was worshiped not for her abilities but for her physicality. She exists frozen in time, always young, always vulnerable, always available. Her most constant visual representation is one of insatiability: over the subway grate, unable to control even the white dress that whips around her head. On the printed page, writers grapple with their inabilities to remove her from the one-dimensional construct of woman as sex object, while at the same time they struggle to give her the voice she never had. During her lifetime she may have been just an object of desire, but for the postmodern writer, the object speaks and the reader listens. One of the strongest voices for Marilyn comes from poet Judy Grahn. She provides Marilyn with a literal escape from the grave, not a resurrection but a liberation:

I have come to claim / Marilyn Monroe's body / for the sake of my own / dig it up, hand it over, / cram it in this paper sack.[8]

Grahn takes Marilyn back from manipulation and hype. Her adoration is for the woman under the skin. The men who populate the poem are the voyeurs, the keepers of the male gaze which they willingly transpose to any female body:

The reporters are furious, they're asking me questions / what right does a woman have to Marilyn Monroe's body? and what / am I doing for lunch? They think I / mean to eat you. Their teeth are lurid / and they want to pose me, leaning / on the shovel nude. Don't squint / But when one of the reporters comes too close / I beat him, bust his camera / with your long, smooth thigh / and with your lovely knucklebone / I break his eye.[9]

Grahn allows Marilyn to fight back after death, to bust cameras and break the eyes of those who see only the facade. Some of the writings about Marilyn focus on her relationship with John F. Kennedy. The nature of the relationship has itself become something of a myth: whether or not there was a relationship of any kind during life, it has become a paramount relationship to Marilyn in the afterlife. Sam Staggs in his book *MMII: The Return of Marilyn Monroe* uses the familiar story line of Marilyn and Kennedy and a plot by the government. But Staggs' Marilyn doesn't commit suicide, she fakes it. Marilyn gets away. No longer Norma Jeane, no longer Marilyn, but now Georgia, she has her mind set on being a serious actress and garners a lively following of fans as a cabaret singer. But not everything in her life is serious. Staggs allows Georgia to be Marilyn once more as she enters a look-alike contest. As she is announced and her eyes light up she goes to the microphone:

> *"My friends . . . I was scared to death to come here tonight . . . afraid you might say, 'Who does that girl think she is trying to be Marilyn Monroe?' But as soon as I felt all that love in your hearts, well I wasn't frightened anymore." She paused while the audience responded. "You've made my day. In fact, you've made my life . . . I'd like to sing for you."*[10]

Her rousing rendition of "Diamonds Are a Girl's Best Friend" wins her the contest and some peace of mind. For some writers, Marilyn is the avenue of escape. As with Elvis, there is a need to assume the physical representation of the icon. Female protagonists become convinced that they have learned from the mistakes of the idol; they will replicate the life, assume the role as well as the physical appearance of the icon and get it right. Women use Marilyn to escape: if she could manage to extricate her life from the humdrum then they should be able to. Even in the realm of the written word, the visual image of Marilyn captivates. In Rosanne Daryl Thomas' *The Angel Carver*, the character Lucille is overwhelmed by the visual icon:

She reached out for a postcard of Marilyn Monroe. Now, that was famous. On damn near every forty-five-cent postcard rack in damn near every drugstore Lucille had ever been in, there she was, Marilyn Monroe, her eyes half shut, her lips wide open, twisting this way and that. In black and white and in color. Everybody wanted her. . . . She paid for the postcard and boarded the bus. She was going to be Marilyn. That was that.[11]

The written word redefines and articulates that which is visual. While our mythic images stare down at us from billboards and movie screens, writers construct new meanings from what they witness. And the stories keep coming. For writers today, Elvis has become a new Zeus, the god of a simple myth, proof that nice guys can finish first. Marilyn is the Aphrodite of our all-consuming consumer society, the sex kitten we all want to love, protect, and exploit. We adore both figures, the touch-stones that remind us who we are and where we can go.

Cameron Jamie (b. 1969). *Drawing of Elvis (Portrait)*. 1993. Ink on rice grain, ⅛ x ¾ x ⅛".
Courtesy of the artist and Robert Berman Gallery, Santa Monica.

Joanne Stephens (b. 1933). *Homage to Elvis.* 1991. Mixed media, 84 x 43 x 21".
Courtesy of the artist.

Jeffrey Vallance (b. 1955). *Elvis Shroud (Elvis Died [on the Toilet] While Reading a Book on the Shroud of Turin)*. 1992. Mixed media, 12¼ x 10¼".
Courtesy of the artist and Rosamund Felsen Gallery, Los Angeles.

Elvis would take one of his dozens of brightly colored scarves, position it around his neck for a few seconds, just enough time to soak in a small portion of sweat, and then repeatedly cast these products into the audience in a climactic ceremony suggestive of the distribution of Holy Eucharist.
Elvis died, on the toilet, while reading a book on the Shroud of Turin. His body, having fallen to the floor, was found in a fetal position in his bathroom. . . . According to the book Elvis *by Albert Goldman, after an exhaustive three-hour autopsy, the corpse of Elvis Aaron Presley was wrapped in a paper shroud.*
Jeffrey Vallance

Jeffrey Vallance (b. 1955). *Elvis Sweatcloth I.* 1993. Sweat on satin, 22 x 22".
Courtesy of the artist and Rosamund Felsen Gallery, Los Angeles.

GRACELAND AS LOCUS SANCTUS[1]

Gary Vikan

PROLOGUE: ELVIS AS SAINT[2]

So that the reader not stop at "saint" Elvis, a notion explicitly sanctioned not only by the tabloids[3] but also by the *Washington Post*[4], the following points should be born in mind:

- that saints, as charismatic mediating agents between our everyday world and remote and powerful spiritual forces, have existed in all religions, and outside conventional religion as well;

- that within Christianity, *de jure* canonization, as now practiced by the Vatican, was a development of the second millennium, and that the Orthodox Church still follows a practice closer to the *de facto* form of canonization which dominated early Christianity, whereby a saint was informally "elected" to sainthood by the collective belief and actions of his followers;

- that Christianity has allowed for saints of vastly varying backgrounds and life-styles, including those despised by their contemporaries;

- that there is a profound difference between the image of the saint held dear by his followers, and the historical reality of the individual, who may not ever have existed;

- and finally, that even within the conventional topology of western saints, comprising martyrs, confessors, ascetics, etc., Elvis, in the eyes of his ardent fans, has his place as a "martyr."

The last point is abundantly clear from even a brief survey of Elvis *vita* literature, such as May Mann's *Elvis, Why Won't They Leave You Alone?* in which we learn the King's last thoughts as he lay dying on the floor of his bathroom: "This must be like what Jesus suffered."[5] Purged from the singer's factual life history are any references to drug abuse, obesity, or paranoic violence. The *vitae*, most of which constitute an extended *apologia* responding to Albert Goldman's damning portrait of Elvis,[6] speak instead of a dirt-poor southern boy who rose to fame and glory, of the love of a son for his mother, of humility and generosity, and of superhuman achievement in the face of adversity. They emphasize Elvis' profound spiritualism and his painful, premature death—a death described as coming at the hands of his own fans, whose merciless demands for Elvis entertainment exhausted and ultimately killed Elvis the entertainer ("uppers" to prepare for a concert, "downers" to get necessary rest afterwards). In their eyes, he had died for them, and any further revelations of his seeming debauchery would, ironically, only reconfirm and intensify their image of his suffering. The stickiness of the word "saint" may be avoided entirely by adopting Max Weber's non-religious, value-neutral terminology, which centers instead on the word charisma ("gift"). Weber identified the charismatic as possessing "a certain quality of an individual personality by virtue of which he is set apart from ordinary men and treated as endowed with supernatural, superhuman, or at least specifically exceptional powers or qualities."[7] Significantly, this extraordinary individual is identifiable not by any specific behavioral or physical characteristics, but rather by the impact he has on others, by how he is "treated as endowed" by his followers. This "affectual action" definition (Weber's term) is especially critical for "saints" whose life-styles strike nonfollowers as inappropriate, since what counts is not saintlike performance, but audience reception and reaction. Again, the "saint" need never, in fact, have existed, for like

Mickey Mouse or the legendary Saint Christopher, he is created and re-created to suit his evolving clientele. Weber's value-neutral approach to charisma shifts emphasis away from the source of the charismatic "gift," as a grace from God or as a reward for an exemplary life, to its recognition. This allows for the existence among the ranks of charismatics of the likes of Jesús Malverde, a mustachioed brigand who was hanged as a bandit in Culiacán, Mexico, in 1909, but who today is venerated there as a saint, with his own chapel-shrine, icons, and votives, and an impressive list of attributed miracles.[8]

Miracle-working was part of the "charisma package" that came with the early Christian saint; this, after all, was what saints were supposed to do. By contrast, the charisma of Elvis the superhuman entertainer included miracle-working only as one of its various potentialities, one of its possible "exceptional powers" (Weber's characterization). Elvis demonstrated the possession of

George Hirose (b. 1957). *Elvis Birthplace, Tupelo, Mississippi, 1990.* 1990.
Oil on photograph, 15½ x 22½". Courtesy of the artist.

I now live in Memphis, where, of course, Graceland is located and Elvis is truly king. Recently, the city erected a civic center in the form of a pyramid. So there you have it, the birthplace, the tomb, the king, all in one.
Greely Myatt

Greely Myatt (b. 1952). *Birthplace of the King.* 1985. Lead, cement, earth, and paint,
15 x 22 x 26". Courtesy of the artist.

charisma through his initial phenomenal success as an entertainer (1955–1957); this "gift" he had in fact earned through his own on-stage and record-industry performance, and its potentiality was then multivalent and unrealized. From that point on, though, through the dismal movie years of the 1960s and the increasingly degenerate Vegas years of the 1970s, Elvis was endowed by his fans with inalienable charisma, and gradually he, together with his inner circle, began to cultivate its latent spiritual and miraculous potentialities. Eventually, Elvis became an acknowledged healer and a self-proclaimed messenger from God. Larry Geller, Elvis' hairdresser and spiritualist, discusses both qualities:

Elvis . . . was interested in telepathy, healing through touch and a number of other phenomena that are only now being scientifically studied.

I once saw Elvis heal a man who was having a heart attack. Another time Elvis treated Jerry Shilling after he had taken a nasty spill on his motorcycle and was unable to move. "The next thing I knew," Jerry said later, "I woke up the following morning healed."

In the seventies . . . I witnessed hundreds of concertgoers carrying their sick and crippled children to the stage and crying out, "Elvis, please touch my baby," or "Elvis, just hold her for a minute."

In Elvis' mind, his life was being directed divinely. . . . And he truly felt that he was chosen to be here now as a modern-day savior, a Christ.

[Elvis recounts:] "Think back when I had that experience in the desert. I didn't only see Jesus' picture in the clouds—Jesus Christ literally exploded in me. Larry, it was me! I was Christ."[9]

Some of Elvis' posthumous miracles were gathered by clinical psychiatrist Raymond A. Moody, Jr., in *Elvis: After Life*,[10] and these are supplemented almost weekly by the tabloids. Elvis appears to a small-town policeman, helping him locate a runaway son by revealing a vision of the Los Angeles rooming house where, in fact, the boy turns up a few days later. Elvis receives into paradise a young girl dying of complications from Down's Syndrome, just as she utters her last words, "Here comes Elvis!" Elvis mostly comforts and guides, but sometimes he heals. "Elvis' Picture Has Cured Me of Cancer!" shouts the headline in the *Weekly World News.*[11]

GRACELAND AS *LOCUS SANCTUS*[12]

The saint has his holy place; this is how we know him for who he is and how we know where to find him, and this, in part, is how he has traditionally effected his miraculous powers on earth. The holy place has existed since the early centuries of Christianity; the Latins called it *locus sanctus* and the Greeks *hagios topos*, but for both the meaning was the same. And for the faithful, its physical attraction was intense: a *locus sanctus* presupposed pilgrimage, pilgrimage required a *locus sanctus*.

A holy place could be the home of an important relic, like the chair in which the Virgin sat during the Annunciation, or the site of miraculous waters, like the leper-curing Baths of Elijah; or it could be the setting of some major religious event, like the Nativity or the Crucifixion. But outside the Holy Land, where the Old and New Testaments dominated the sacred landscape, a *locus sanctus* usually turned out to be the home of a saint. It might be the place of a saint still living (a "holy man") or, more likely, the place of his bodily remains, sealed in a tomb or reliquary and enshrined in elaborate architecture: the martyr ("witness") for Christ enshrined in his *martyrion*.

The tiny rock-cut Tomb of Christ in the Church of the Holy Sepulchre in Jerusalem has always been Christianity's most important *locus sanctus*.[13] Its shrine, a vast complex of churches, courtyards, and colonnades, now mostly destroyed, was built in the early fourth century by Emperor Constantine. Nearly as important is the Basilica of St. Peter in Rome, originally also fourth century in date, with its bones of the Prince of the Apostles, and very important too, though only from a much later period, is the cathedral of Chartres, near Paris, with its Veil of the Virgin Mary. There are thousands more, of every description and size, from those that dominate an entire city to those hidden away in a forest or isolated on a mountaintop, from those commanding international pilgrimage to those drawing pious traffic only from a nearby village. Just a fraction date from the first millennium of Christianity, and a smaller proportion still is to be found on the sacred real estate of Christ and the Apostles.[14]

In the desert hills north of Santa Fe is one of Christianity's newer holy places: El Sanctuario de Chimayó.[15] Unassuming by medieval standards, its shrine is not a cathedral but a simple adobe chapel, its "witness" not holy bones or sacred cloth but a kettle-size hole in its clay floor. Chimayó is a *locus sanctus* because in the early nineteenth century, during Holy Week, a local Penetente brother discovered a partially buried crucifix there of Our Lord of Esquípulas, and each time that he dug it up and carried it to the church at Santa Cruz, it returned of its own accord to that spot, to the hole that has ever since given forth miracle-working *tierra bendita*. Now each year on Good Friday, thirty thousand or more make the pilgrimage to El Sanctuario, because they believe, as Christians have nearly always believed, that the sacred power of a saintly body or a miraculous event literally charges its physical surroundings with holiness.

But what is now taken for granted by hundreds of millions of Christians worldwide was not always part of Christian belief. Initially, the Holy Land was simply Palestine, and Jerusalem was only one among many locations in Palestine which bore witness to the historical truth of Christ the man. Constantine's act of unearthing and enshrining the Tomb of Christ in the early fourth century betrays a critical transformation in attitude, after which the documentary dimension of Jerusalem and Palestine, and of important Christian sites and objects generally, was superseded by their spiritual dimension, by the belief that they bore sacred power and miracle-working potential.[16] The eighth-century Byzantine theologian John of Damascus explained the sanctity and thus the attraction of the True Cross, and, by extension, of the *martyrion* that once enshrined it: "So, then, that honorable and most truly venerable tree upon which Christ offered Himself as a sacrifice for us is itself to be adored, because it has been sanctified by contact with the sacred body and blood."[17]

Unlike the tourist, who goes places mostly to see, the pilgrim has a distinctly tactile notion of travel. Paulinus of Nola (d. 431) observed that "the principal motive which draws people to Jerusalem is the desire to see and touch the places where Christ was present in the body."[18] As early Christianity came to accept the notion that the holy was susceptible to concentration in places, people, and things (the "objectification of charisma"), it inevitably came to accept the corollary notion that the power of that localized holy was susceptible to retransfer through contagion. Christ is nailed to the cross and the cross is infused with the power of his sanctity; Christ's (now) relic-cross, the "True Cross," comes into contact with earth and that earth becomes similarly empowered; when the pilgrim takes away a small packet of that holy earth, he takes away the sacred power of Christ. In the vocabulary of contemporary travel diaries and saints' lives, this is the pilgrim's *eulogia* or "blessing."[19] The diary of an anonymous pilgrim from Piacenza in northern Italy, who made his trip to Jerusalem around 570, records the practice of bringing earth into Christianity's preeminent contact relic, the Holy Sepulchre, so that "those who go in [may] take some as a blessing."[20] In Jerusalem today one may still buy little packets of earth labeled "from Calvary" and small vials of oil that are said to have touched the Tomb of Christ. In the eyes of faith, the tomb of a saint was (and is) understood to be much more than mere tangible evidence of the historical reality of that individual; it is a sacred point of intersection between the physical and the metaphysical, between earth and heaven. The soul of the saint is believed to dwell there, and in being nearby, one is in the company of "the invisible friend."[21] Conversely, to be separated from the tomb was to be apart from one's friend, and the remedy for that was pilgrimage.

TOURIST AS PILGRIM

Pilgrimage has always been intertwined with tourism, even in the days of the early Christian saints.[22] True, major biblical sites and the shrines of famous saints were the great attractions that then set the Christian world in motion, and each, by itself, would have been worthy of a trip. Yet once near sacred soil, the pious traveler would have been drawn to a wide range of lesser attractions, not all of which would be religious. The pilgrim from Piacenza, on his journey toward Jerusalem around the year 570, kept a detailed diary from the point he entered the Holy Land, at Ptolemais (modern Acco). He stopped first at Diocaesarea (modern Zippori) to see the chair in which the Virgin sat during the Annunciation, and then went on to Cana to touch the two surviving water jugs whose contents Christ had miraculously turned to wine. From there he was off four or so miles to Nazareth where, among other things, he saw preserved in the local synagogue the book in which Christ, as a child, had written his ABCs. These sacred detours substantially dictated this pilgrim's zigzag path toward Jerusalem, yet he was occasionally drawn as well to sightsee such local curiosities as the magical, birth-ensuring geodes on Mount Carmel, the huge one-pound dates at Jericho (which he picked and took home), the beautiful Jewesses in Nazareth, and the Ethiopians in the Negev, who "had their nostrils split, their ears cut, boots on their feet, and rings on their toes."[23]

Undoubtedly most of the seven hundred thousand annual visitors to Graceland come in the tourist mode, even if some among them may eventually experience there a vague sense of "localized

Guillaume Bijl (b. 1946). *Composition Trouvée*. 1990. Plaster, glass, mixed media, 102 x 85½ x 20".
Courtesy of Jack Shainman Gallery, New York. © Guillaume Bijl/VAGA, New York 1994.

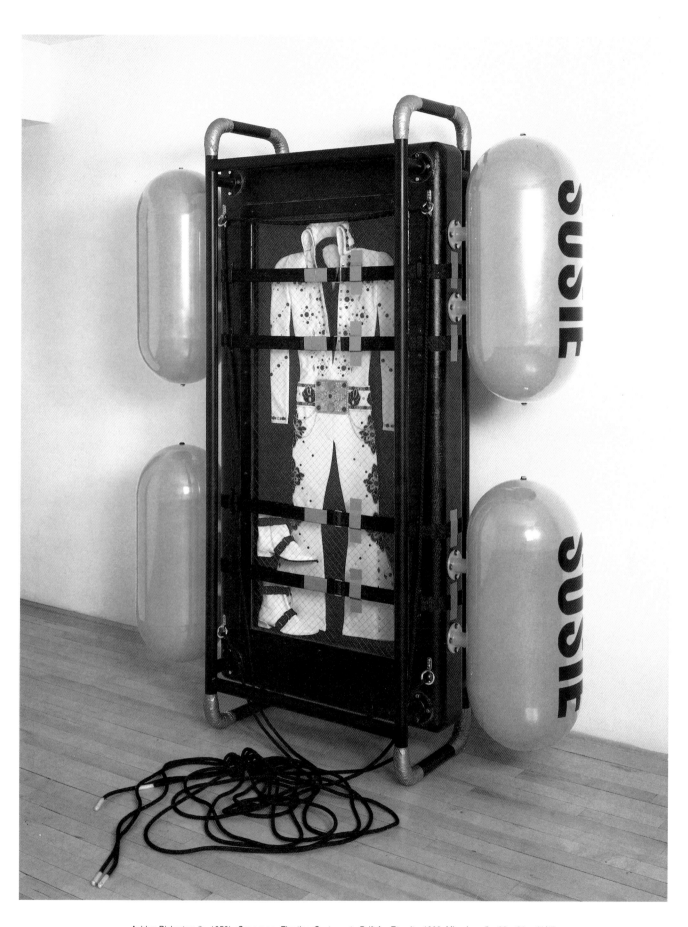

Ashley Bickerton (b. 1959). *Seascape: Floating Costume to Drift for Eternity*. 1992. Mixed media, 92 x 81 x 41½".
Courtesy of Sonnabend Gallery, New York.

sacred." And certainly, many among that minority whose initial travel aims are closer to those of the Piacenza pilgrim might still be distracted by such local Memphis curiosities as Mud Island, Beale Street, and the baby-back ribs at Corky's. The trick is to disentangle the pilgrim from the tourist, both as a statistically identifiable group, and as a qualitatively identifiable attitude.[24] It is the contention of this article that Graceland is essentially of a type with the medieval *locus sanctus*. Since the *locus sanctus* is identifiable not by any single set of physical characteristics, but rather by what people do in relationship to it (Weber's "affectual action" notion), so the relative degree of "holy-place-ness" of Graceland can only be so defined. The history of religiously motivated travel to holy places inside and outside of Christianity suggests several activity-defined criteria for identifying the pilgrim, and thus, by extension, the holy place.

When does the pilgrim go?

The travel schedule of the tourist is dictated primarily by vacation time and the seasons, whereas that of the pilgrim is dictated by the yearly calendar of holy days associated with the sanctification of the destination site. The Piacenza pilgrim goes to the Jordan River on January 6, the day upon which the Baptism of Christ is commemorated there; similarly, since the earliest centuries of Christianity, Bethlehem has been the preferred pilgrimage destination for December 25, and Jerusalem for Holy Week. This is so because in the eyes of faith the holy day, within the unending yearly cycle of sacred remembrances, is the occasion of complete time collapse between the now and the then. To be in the Church of the Holy Sepulchre on any day is to be proximate to the sacred, but to be there on Good Friday is to be there at the Crucifixion. Of course, sacred time obtains independent of sacred locale in Easter services worldwide, but to be in Jerusalem for those services is to compound the intensity of the spiritual encounter. Sacred experience is, in this respect, a function of the where and the when.

Disney World is fully booked in mid-March because this is when school children have their spring vacation and when the weather in Florida is especially attractive. By contrast, Chimayó is most active during Holy Week, and Graceland's peak activity time is always in mid-August, in that special "holy week," Elvis International Tribute Week, surrounding the anniversary of Elvis' death, on August 16.[25] Contributing to a powerful sensation of "time collapse" around Graceland then are the steamy weather, the nighttime crowds on Elvis Presley Boulevard, the ubiquitous Elvis imitators and impersonators, ever-present Elvis music, and periodic rebroadcast, on radio station 56-WHBQ, of the heart-wrenching interview with Vernon Presley on the afternoon of August 16, 1977, shortly after Elvis had been pronounced dead.

The appearance of the Elvis grave shrine in mid-August and the quality and tempo of activity around it are very different from the non-holiday season. During Tribute Week alone there are fifty thousand visitors to Graceland, and one senses immediately that as a group they stand apart; these make up the most concentrated pool of Elvis Friends, and these, disproportionately, account for the pilgrimage activity described below.[26]

What is the nature of the pilgrim's itinerary?

The organizing criterion for a tourist's itinerary might be Civil War monuments, theme parks, three-star restaurants or campgrounds. By contrast, the pilgrim organizes his itinerary around ancillary holy places, while all the time maintaining strong directionality toward the paramount sacred destination. We have already encountered this in the diary of the Piacenza pilgrim, who, like most other Holy Land travelers then and since, made use of specially tailored maps and guidebooks. His counterpart during Tribute Week will likely have, in addition to the site map for Graceland, the Red Line "Map and Guide, with Historical Addresses to Elvis Presley." This will point him southward on Route 78 toward the Elvis birth shrine in Tupelo, and in Memphis, toward such important local sites as Lauderdale Courts (Elvis' first Memphis home), Lansky Brothers (Elvis' clothier), Sun Records (Elvis' first recording studio), and Chenault's Restaurant, "where Elvis and his guests would have hamburgers in the sealed off back room." Everywhere on the tour there will be an intense feeling of Elvis' "presence," heightened by specificity of place and time, and by relics; one sits on the very stoop at Lauderdale Courts where Elvis once sat as he sang to his first girlfriend, Betty McMann, and in Humes High School, one touches the Elvis football uniform, and then one writes on the Elvis blackboard. Again, the Piacenza pilgrim:

Three miles further on [from Diocaesarea] we came to Cana, where the Lord attended the wedding, and we actually reclined on the couch [where the Lord had reclined]. On it (undeserving though I am)

I wrote the names of my parents. . . . Of the water-pot [in which Jesus changed water to wine] two are still there, and I filled one of them up with wine and lifted it up to my shoulder.[27]

Characteristically, the August Graceland pilgrim travels a greater distance than the June Graceland tourist and expends greater effort; almost certainly, this will not have been the first visit. Paradigmatic, though extreme, is Pete Ball, the "EP"-tattooed London laborer who between 1982 and 1987 came to Graceland fifty-three times, all the while never stopping anywhere else in the United States.[28]

What is the pilgrim's relationship to his fellow travelers?

Nothing could be more unlike the anonymity and dispassion of tourist travel than the intense bonding that takes place among the faithful during Tribute Week. Anthropologists speak of the *communitas* of pilgrimage, and emphasize the liminoid nature of the experience, which like a rite of passage takes the pilgrim out of the flow of his day-to-day existence and leaves him in some measure transformed.[29] Nowhere are community and bonding more apparent than at the Days Inn Motel on Brooks Road, between Graceland and the airport, which each year sponsors the Tribute Week Elvis Window Decorating Contest. *Communitas* begins in the parking lot, with its rows of Cadillacs and Lincolns bearing Elvis vanity plates, and it continues around the pool, where pilgrims gather to drink Budweiser and reminisce.

One senses in the poolside conversation of Tribute Week the inevitable evolution of recalled anecdote from those relating to the living Elvis to those relating to extraordinary events surrounding *post mortem* August gatherings. This, too, must have had its counterpart in the early Christian world, as those pilgrims and locals with memories of the living saint died off. The texture of conversation at the Days Inn is now weighted toward stories of extraordinary pilgrimage (long distance, great sacrifice), although these are interwoven with accounts of the seemingly supernatural, the stuff of future Elvis *miracula*. One such account was later documented in the Fall 1988 *Elvis Fever* fan club quarterly (Baltimore), under the heading "Report from Memphis":

[We] went back to Graceland [from the Days Inn] for the Candlelight Service. As we were sitting across from Graceland waiting to get in line (we learned last year the hard way to wait until after midnight to get in line), my sister and I noticed that there was only one star in the sky and it was directly over Elvis' grave. Understand this was the third year that this has occurred. It gave you an eerie feeling.

Group identity is acknowledged through Elvis clothing, jewelry, and in some cases, tattoos. There is first-name familiarity among the "we," and an openness to new members, who are initiated through friendly interrogation: "How many times have you been to Graceland?" "How many concerts did you attend?" "How many Elvis videos do you own?" Elvis' motto in life was "Taking Care of Business," and the unspoken motto among the *post mortem* "we" is "Taking Care of Elvis." The despised "other" extends well beyond the circle of Colonel Parker, Albert Goldman, and Geraldo, to include Priscilla, whose infidelity is believed by most to have destroyed Elvis' will to live, and who in any event is generally acknowledged as having been "uppity" and to have wrecked Graceland by redecorating it Hollywood-style.

As the "living Elvis" oral tradition of Tribute Week is institutionalized in the annual Humes High Symposium, featuring, among others, Elvis' belt maker and horse trainer (Mike McGregor), drummer (D. J. Fontana), and cook (Nancy Rook), so the "Taking Care of Elvis" tradition is institutionalized in the yearly Fan Appreciation Social at the Memphis Airport Hilton. Here Elvis Friends petition for Elvis stamps and Elvis holidays, and then gather to grill the powers within the circle of "we" on the present state of the Elvis Image. A report in a local fan newsletter on a recent Fan Social included the following characteristic exchange:

The fans let Jack Soden [Elvis Presley Enterprises Executive Director] and the Graceland Executives know how upset they were by the movie "Elvis and Me." Mr. Soden's only reply was he was also upset by it, but they really did not have control over what was finally shown. If they had, it would have been stopped. Mr. Soden was also questioned as to why Graceland was not responding to the "Elvis is Alive" thing. His main reply was that Graceland did not want to fuel the publicity by replying and were hoping it would just go away. But it hasn't. Does Graceland have to dig up Elvis' body to prove that he died?[30]

James B. Pink (b. 1945). *Resurrection*. 1993. Mixed-media drawing, 44 x 30".
Collection of Ellis M. Pryce-Jones, Las Vegas.

Resurrection *is one of a series of pictures begun in 1992 entitled* Elvis Sightings. *In these pieces Elvis is recognized shopping for groceries or buying his commemorative stamp at a post office disguised as Groucho Marx, not wanting to be recognized after being dead for so many years. Many times these sightings take place in a historical context related to a pictorial place in art history.*

The iconography of the rabbits and tree with a bird perched on its limb are symbols that are represented in a painting by Giovanni Bellini entitled Christ Blessing, *painted in 1500. Replacing the figure of Christ with the image of Elvis gives an authenticity of historical reference in that Elvis, like Christ, has risen in a similar manner.*

A 7-Eleven sign in Elvis' resurrection replaces the city of Jerusalem in Christ Blessing, *signifying a difference in time and space, physically as well as culturally.*

The incised lyrics from the voice of Elvis are Christlike scars that depict his pain. For his journey through time I felt it appropriate to robe Elvis in a leather jacket and motorcycle hat; the look of the leader of the Wild Ones, a time traveler, a sky pilot, the elusive image that continues to resurrect throughout our culture.

James B. Pink

Ted Faiers (1908–1975). *Rendezvous.* 1977. Acrylic on canvas, 61½ x 72¼".
Courtesy Tennessee State Museum.

The universally acknowledged, often-repeated aim of this is to present the world with a positive image of Elvis, "the real Elvis."

What does the pilgrim do when he gets there?

The behavior profile of the August Graceland pilgrim will be quite different from that of the June Graceland tourist. While the latter's (substantially dispassionate) experience will likely be restricted to a few hours, and center on the Graceland Mansion tour, the former's will probably extend over several days, and will be distinctly "di-polar," both by location and by tone. One pole, already discussed, will be the Days Inn poolside, or wherever peer-group bonding and "liminality" are at that moment most attractive, and the other will be the Meditation Garden, and specifically, the Elvis grave. The former, obviously, is a social experience, whereas the latter is thoroughly private, and devotional; the mood at poolside will be festive and at the Fan Social feisty, whereas at graveside, it will be somber.

The two poles of the mid-August experience, social and devotional, merge in the ritual which is the highlight of Tribute Week: the Annual Candlelight Service. The "order" of the service, which commences outside Melody Gates at 10:00 p.m., includes a Bible reading, silent prayer, spirituals (sung by Elvis over strategically placed loudspeakers), and a homily based on a song or a value associated with Elvis. A few years back the homily was based on the song "Always on My Mind," and it focused on the shared guilt implicit in the notion of Elvis' "martyrdom." Recited tearfully to a hushed crowd of more than ten thousand, it included these revealing sentiments:

Looking back through the years as we take this moment to remember—I have regrets. I regret all of those little things that I should have said and done to let you know how much you mean to me, Elvis. . . .

A thousand souls joined together in harmony, as we are tonight, can only hope to return some of the love that Elvis has shared with each and every one of us. Though we are united as one, we know that Elvis belongs to each and every one of us exclusively. . . .

Elvis . . . left us all with a very special gift—the gift of his love. Elvis gave unselfishly of himself to all of us, but did we, his fans, give as much of ourselves to him?[31]

Following a group-sing of "Can't Help Falling in Love," the song with which Elvis closed his concerts in later years, the Melody Gates swing open and the candlelight procession begins to snake its way up the driveway to the Meditation Garden and the graveside. The last pilgrim will lay his votive rose on the bronze tomb slab well after 2:00 a.m. The vigil or evening service before the commemoration day of a saint or an important biblical event has been part of *locus sanctus* pilgrimage ritual for more than fifteen centuries, as has the link between fire and "imminent presence" at holy graveside. Its earliest and still most familiar manifestation is Holy Fire, the miraculous flame marking the Resurrection of Christ; it comes as the culmination of the pascal vigil, at the stroke of midnight between Holy Saturday and Easter Sunday.

What does the pilgrim take away?

The tourist and the pilgrim will both take things home from Graceland, but their mix of "souvenirs" will be different. True, the Tribute Week visitor will likely buy a few of the traditional sorts of tourist trinkets available in the shops across from Graceland Mansion, but his real interest will be in what is colloquially called "Elvis stuff"—which means, at least in part, relics (such as the sweaty concert scarf that has never been washed). Although the souvenir shops along Elvis Presley Boulevard sometimes stock prepackaged *eulogia*-like items, such as Graceland earth, and Uncle Vester is still there to sign and instantly "relicize" copies of *A Presley Speaks,* formal trade in this sort of material during Tribute Week centers mostly on the Annual Elvis Presley Benefit Auction at the Whitehaven United Methodist Church on Elvis Presley Boulevard. Some informal trading takes place on the sidewalks of Graceland Plaza, where, for example, Elvis' classmate Sid McKinney could be found during a recent Tribute Week hawking his 1953 Humes High Yearbook, with Elvis handwritten dedication, for 4,500 dollars. But mostly, Elvis stuff is bought, sold, and exchanged in the rooms of the Days Inn and other motels nearby, where the Elvis Friends congregate.[32] And while much of the material available these days—Elvis clocks, lamps, and placemats—does not technically qualify as "relic," since it has never had direct Elvis contact, some of it does, including the ubiquitous trays of original Elvis concert photographs, which are valued much less as documents of specific events than as almost-tactile appropriations of Elvis, as his handprint or footprint might be.[33]

What does the pilgrim leave behind?

The Christian pilgrim not only took something away from the *locus sanctus* (a relic, an *eulogia*), he usually left something behind. It might be an elaborate, custom-made image set up in a prominent place in the *martyrion* to acknowledge publicly the pilgrim's encounter with his spiritual "friend," or it might be an anonymous personal item, like the "bracelets, rings, tiaras, plaited girdles, and belts," which according to the Piacenza pilgrim were draped "in vast numbers" over the Tomb of Christ— or it might be a simple greeting or prayer hastily drawn on any available surface, like that in the Chapel of St. Vartan beneath the Church of the Holy Sepulchre, which shows a pilgrim's boat and bears the words "O Lord, we have come."[34] Each is a votive, and in its various forms a votive could serve at once as a record of the pilgrim's visit, as a perpetuation of his devotional contact with his "friend," and as a thank-you for a blessing received or anticipated.[35]

At Graceland there are two main types of votives and each has its own characteristic setting. The first type is found mostly in the Meditation Garden; its primary medium is the flower, and it usually is based on an iconographic conceit evocative of an Elvis quality, motto or event, or of the geographical origin of the pilgrim who dedicated it. Sometimes an explicit typological identity between Elvis and pilgrim is evoked, specific to place (Meditation Garden) and time (Tribute Week). Elvis, with head bowed, is presented among flowers, and against the evoked backdrop of the hymn "In the Garden," which begins: "I come to the garden alone / while the dew is still on the roses / and the voice I hear. . . ."[36] Elvis is thus one and the same with the Tribute Week pilgrim, who comes to the Meditation Garden alone during the dawn "free walk-up period," from 6:00 to 7:30 a.m. But on its simplest level, the Elvis votive is the artificial rose sold from the huge cardboard boxes at the 7-Eleven across Elvis Presley Boulevard in the days leading up to August 15, and dedicated at graveside by the thousands that evening, as each Elvis Friend reaches his destination.

The second type of Graceland votive is the graffito message, the counterpart to the fourth-century sketch in the Chapel of St. Vartan. (Recall that the Piacenza pilgrim wrote the names of his parents on the couch at Cana.) In the early Christian *locus sanctus* such impromptu votive communications were common. Some called for or acknowledged help from the "friend," and some simply recorded a name, either of the pilgrim himself, or else of a relative or friend who could not make the journey. In either case the intention was the same: to perpetuate the pilgrim's "presence" at the holy place, and more specifically, to actualize his communication with the saint commemorated there, as later pilgrims would read his words, and perhaps even recite them aloud.

The rules laid down by Elvis Presley Enterprises are explicit and strict; nothing can be touched, and graffiti is of course forbidden, except in one location: the Fans' Memorial Wall. Here messages are not merely tolerated, they are actively encouraged, by occasional sandblasting, which frees up the limited writing space, and by the frontage road off Elvis Presley Boulevard, which allows the mobile pilgrim to pull off in his car and scrawl his message in magic marker without upsetting traffic. The Wall is simply that: a pinkish-yellow fieldstone barrier about six feet high and 175 yards long, setting off the Graceland complex from the road. It is illegal to scale this barrier, but one is encouraged to write on it, and at least ten thousand Elvis Friends do so every year.

The messages, with a few cynical exceptions—"Elvie Baby, Can I have your doc's #?"—carry conviction. Some, echoing the *vitae*, are angry and combative, and addressed to the "other"— "The King never did drugs"—but most are sweet and sentimental, and addressed to the King. Beyond the hundreds of simple confessions of eternal love and devotion ("Elvis, I miss you and love you tender—Loving you, Annette"), there are scores of messages carrying raw, seemingly spontaneous evocations of sorrow or loss: "8-16-77 is the saddest day of / my life. I was too young to realize / it at the time. I was ten. / Love / Ralph." Others, in much the same tone, offer thanks for Elvis' spiritual intervention: "Elvis / Thanks / for all you helped me through. / I wouldn't be me / without you. / See you in heaven. / I love you / Carla." And there are many, like the graffito in the Chapel of St. Vartan, that evoke the very act of pilgrimage: "Fm London— Memphis / Too young to remember / here to respect / Alan, Tim, Lisa & Bev." Within just a few feet of one another are messages in Japanese, Spanish, French, German, Greek, and Russian, as well as those written in English by pilgrims identifying themselves as Swedes, Austrians, and Brazilians. And everywhere, there is reference to multiple visits, either promises to return or, more frequently, allusions to past pilgrimages: "We love you Elvis. Carol Horn, Caroline Kuszuk. 8-15-86, '87, '88, '89—Chicago." There are votives

John Marc Peckham (b. 1960). *Lights, Waves, Bows, Thunder.* 1992. Oil on birch panel with gold leaf,
3 works, each 36 x 24". Courtesy of the artist.

Joni Mabe (b. 1957). *The Elvis Presley Scrapbook.* 1982. Hardcover book with box, 15½ x 11½ x 3½"; box 18 x 15⅓ x 4¾".
Collection of the Ruth and Marvin Sackner Archive of Concrete and Visual Poetry, Miami Beach.

with overt religious messages, like "Elvis Lives" above a radiating Calvary Cross, and finally, there are votives that capture the very essence of pilgrimage piety, and of Graceland: "I have seen / Graceland, my life is complete. / Miss you terribly / Soren Skovdal."

EPILOGUE: ELVIS AS "AN ICON FOR OUR TIME"

Although the August 1989 Sotheby's catalogue *Rock 'n' Roll and Film Memorabilia,* pictured Elvis on its cover, it included "relics" of many other celebrities, including Marilyn Monroe, whose black stiletto shoes from *Some Like it Hot* (lot 30) were projected to bring a price nearly as high as Elvis' 1976 coney jacket (lot 39). On July 26, 1992, the *New York Times* lead article in the Arts and Leisure Section, entitled "Marilyn's Magic Lingers 30 Years After Her Death," characterized Marilyn Monroe as a "serious icon . . . gifted with a bizarrely passive charisma." As for trading in celebrity earth, this, too, is not unique to Elvis; a Californian claims to have sold twenty thousand packets of dirt from the lawns of Johnny Carson, Shirley MacLaine, Katharine Hepburn, and nearly four dozen other stars for $1.95 each, by mail order and in novelty shops. Elvis' charisma-infused corpse, like that of some Christian saints, required special security, but this has been true as well of all sorts of famous figures in modern times, including dictators: in 1987, on the thirteenth anniversary of his death, thieves broke into Juan Perón's locked tomb and surgically removed his hands.[37] Over the last two decades thousands have made the pilgrimage to gather "sanctified soil" from the gravesite of Jim Morrison in Père-Lachaise cemetery in Paris, and many have left "votive" messages of the Elvis sort. And on the anniversary of John Lennon's death, "Lennon Friends" gather in Manhattan for a candlelight vigil at the assassination site outside the Dakota.

Insofar as the cult of the dead Elvis differs from these, or from that of John Kennedy for that matter, it probably differs more in degree than in kind: fifty thousand gathered at Graceland for the tenth anniversary of Elvis Presley's death, whereas just a few hundred gathered at the Dakota for the tenth anniversary of John Lennon's death; on any given day two thousand or more will pass through Graceland's Meditation Garden, whereas just a couple dozen "Morrison Friends" per day will find his grave in Père-Lachaise.

The analytical model of the Centers for Disease Control may be useful here, since it differentiates among etiology or "cause," phenomenology, which is the aggregate of symptoms as presented in the individual, and epidemiology, which is the pattern of distribution among the general population. What sets the Elvis "affliction" apart is its epidemiology, its sheer scale, and probably also its phenomenology, its intensity as presented in the individual. For an excellent primer in the extremes of the latter, one need only check out Rhino Video's *Mondo Elvis: The Strange Rites & Rituals of the King's Most Devoted Disciples* (Monticello Productions, 1984), to meet Artie "Elvis" Mentz, the EP impersonator who equates his relationship to the King to that of a priest to God, since both are filling in for "someone not there in body."

As for etiology, whether the case study be Graceland or Chimayó, the question of root cause lies beyond the scope of comparative religion and this article, in the realm of social anthropology and psychology. That the idiom of Elvis' charismatic performance might be like that of a pentecostal evangelist,[38] and that the idiom of Graceland pilgrimage might be like that of an early Christian *locus sanctus*, should not be taken to imply and certainly does not require that there be a genealogical link between the cult of Elvis and historical or contemporary Christianity. On the contrary, such resonances suggest that the predisposition toward "charisma objectification" that is their shared inspiration is primal and ahistorical, and that over time and across cultures this predisposition will tend to manifest itself in similar though potentially fully independent ways.

Finally, it is striking that among the inscriptions at Graceland, and in Elvis *vitae* and tabloid literature generally, there is seldom any hint of Elvis as intercessor, even when he is clearly the proximate source of the miraculous, and even when the context is richly flavored with conventional religion.[39] Rarely is God or Jesus ever mentioned, and rarely is there any talk of Elvis as being the recipient of prayer. In this respect, Elvis' "sainthood" is strikingly different from the conventional Christian sort, wherein the role of one's spiritual "friend" as one's advocate before God is always central.

Though, of course, sainthood, either as performed or as acknowledged, is not a constant, even in Christianity; the great martyrs mostly date from before the Peace of the Church (fourth century), and retreating into the desert as an expression of saintly piety went out of fashion more than a millennium ago. As the early Christian saint was a product of and a window upon his world, so also is Elvis Presley. In the words of Elvis Friend Anna Norman, written on the Fans' Memorial Wall: "Elvis, You've become such an icon for our time."

I was drawn to Graceland not for Elvis but for the event itself, for the photographs that I sensed waited there, for the wonderful strangeness of it all, for the new myth.
It was the first anniversary of Elvis' death when I heard the news—thousands of his fans were heading to Memphis, spontaneously, just to be there. So I went, an unwitting pilgrim to the nascent shrine. And I have returned ever since, a birthday here, a deathday there, never often enough, much too often to explain away, always curious as to why they do it, never completely coming to terms with why I do it. Each return is my last, but when I miss two or three in a row I begin to feel disconnected, cut away from events that I need to see and photograph. So I go back and stand by the grave and watch people, some of whom are now my friends, and talk with them about their lives and inevitably wonder about them and about me and about us and wish that I had answers and that I know more about this incredible love and pain and worship spread so easily before me.

Ralph Burns

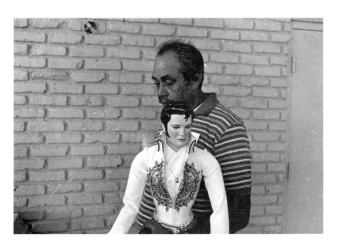 

Ralph Burns (b. 1944). *Untitled* (from *Graceland Series*). 1977–93. Six photographic silver prints, each 11 x 14".
Courtesy of the artist.

Michael Rothenstein (1908–1993). *Marilyn I*. 1978. Woodcut and screenprint, 31¼ x 23".
Courtesy of Angela Flowers Gallery, London.

Mark Lancaster (b. 1938). From *Post-Warhol Souvenirs*. 1987–88.
Oil on canvas, 12 x 10". Courtesy of the artist.

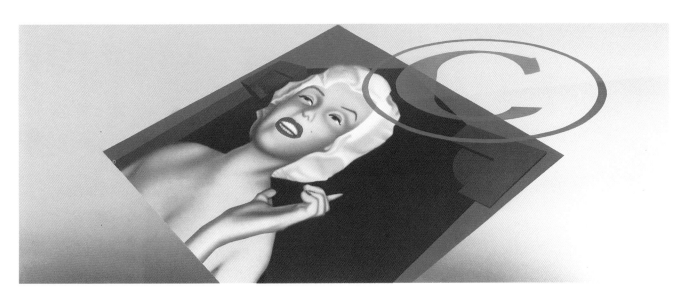

Bernard Joisten (b. 1962). *Remix*. 1988. Acrylic on PVC, Plexiglas, 31¾ x 80¼".
Collection of Nathalie and Laurent Dembert, Paris.

Seymour Howard (b. 1928). *Icon Diptych*. 1993. Acrylic and photocopy, two panels,
each 7⅝ x 7¼". Private collection.

Note to Editors' Statement

1. Later interpretations of art of the fifties and sixties speak of new patterns that were formed as a result of encounters with Buddhism, Taoism, and a variety of other forms of Asian thought. These include Gail Gelburd and Geri DePaoli, *The Transparent Thread: Asian Philosophy in Recent American Art* (Philadelphia: University of Pennsylvania Press, 1990).

Poets, musicians, dancers, and artists, including Jack Kerouac, Allen Ginsberg, Gary Snyder, John Cage, Merce Cunningham, and Martha Graham, each in his or her unique way, formed their world view by the overlay of Asian thought along with other readings in philosophy and modern physics. Artists labeled Abstract Expressionist, Pop, and Funk used these new notions when referring to a potential for spiritual transformation within the ordinary. This new world view had a radically different conception about space/time, subject/object, form/void, yin/yang. It changed the art and the reason for making art. A Zen dictum often repeated by artists and writers, "No one thing more important than the other," gives a clue to a spiritual context of Pop art.

Repetition of ordinary images becomes a mantra with no direct reference to the object pictured. Juxtaposition of ordinary objects, as a Coke can or a stop sign, can become the ground for an experience of enlightenment. After studying Buddhism at a summer session in Colorado in the 1960s at the Jack Kerouac Institute for Disembodied Poets (later called the Naropa Institute), James Rosenquist protested the "dumb critics" who spoke of the back end of a Cadillac as the subject of one of his paintings. He said that he chose such a well-known form because he thought it would be meaningless. The work, he said, was about the powerful potential of emptiness, space/time, form/void. In a taped conversation with Geri DePaoli, the late Robert Arneson said that when these ideas become embedded in your psyche, it gives permission, a leveling, where anything can hold the potential, the spirit. These misunderstandings of artists' motivations have been the critical norm because the radical shift in world view never entered the mainstream of criticism of Pop art.

Note to Millett, "Marilyn, We Hardly Knew You"

1. Kwannon is the designation in Japanese Buddhism for Avalokiteshvara, the Lord Who Looks Down, the embodiment of compassion and wisdom. In India this bodhisattva was represented in male form, but in China and Japan Avalokiteshvara was transformed into a female (In China the name is Kuan-yin) [GDP].

Notes to Heller and Elms, "Elvis Presley: Character and Charisma"

1. Jerry Hopkins, *Elvis, A Biography* (New York: Simon & Schuster, 1971), p. 135.

2. C. Peterson, "The Love That I Feel," *Rock and Roll Roundup,* vol. 1 no. 4 (1957), p. 8.

3. Vernon Presley and N. Anderson, "Elvis," *Good Housekeeping,* vol. 186 no. 1 (January 1978), p. 160.

4. Elvis Presley, recorded interview, Vancouver, 1957.

5. In various preliterate societies, especially in Polynesia and Australasia, the *mana,* or magical power, of the gods is often incorporated in similar fashion by their followers.

6. Pauline Kael, *Taking It All In* (New York: Holt, Rinehart & Winston, 1984), p. 132.

7. Hopkins, pp. 143–44.

8. Hopkins, p. 22.

9. C. R. Jennings, "There'll Always Be an Elvis," *Saturday Evening Post,* vol. 238 (September 11, 1965), p. 78.

10. Mick Farren and P. Marchbank, *Elvis in His Own Words* (London: Omnibus Press, 1977), pp. 30–31.

11. Elaine Dundy, *Elvis and Gladys* (New York: Macmillan, 1985), ch. 3.

12. Dundy, p. 84.

13. Margaret S. Mahler, F. Pine, and A. Bergman, *The Psychological Birth of the Human Infant* (New York: Basic Books, 1975), p. 3.

14. Daniel Stern, *The Interpersonal World of the Human Infant* (New York: Basic Books, 1985).

15. Heinz Kohut, *Restoration of the Self* (New York: International University Press, 1977).

16. Mary D. S. Ainsworth, M. Blehar, E. Waters, and S. Wall, *Patterns of Attachment* (Hillsdale, N.J.: Erlbaum, 1978).

17. Mary D. S. Ainsworth and C. G. Eichberg, "Effects of Infant-Mother Attachment on Mother's Unresolved Loss of an Attachent Figure or Other Traumatic Experience," in *Attachment Across the Life Cycle*, ed. C. M. Parkes, J. Stevenson-Hinde, and P. Marris (New York: Routledge, 1991); Mary Main and E. Hesse, "Parents' Unresolved Traumatic Experiences are Related to Infant Disorganized Attachment Status," in *Attachment in the Preschool Years*, ed. M. T. Greenberg, D. Cicchetti, and E. M. Cummings (Chicago: University of Chicago Press, 1990).

18. Farren and Marchbank, p. 17.

19. Dirk Vellenga and Mick Farren, *Elvis and the Colonel* (New York: Delacorte Press, 1988).

20. Priscilla Beaulieu Presley and P. Harmon, *Elvis and Me* (New York: Putnam, 1985), pp. 285–88.

21. Mardi Horowitz, *States of Mind* (New York: Plenum, 1987).

22. Memphis *Commercial Appeal*, August 16, 1958.

23. Hopkins, p. 82.

24. Saul Friedländer, *History and Psychoanalysis*, trans. Susan Suleiman (New York: Holmes and Meier, 1978).

25. Peter Eicher, *The Elvis Sighting*s (New York: Avon Books, 1993).

Notes to Martin, "Mediating Marilyn: Richard Hamilton's *My Marilyn*"

1. Leo Braudy, "Marilyn, Now an Opera," *International Herald Tribune,* September 15, 1993.

2. Richard Hamilton, *Collected Words*, 1982, p. 65.

3. Thierry de Duve, "The Monochrome and the Blank Canvas," in Serge Guilbaut, ed., *Reconstructing Modernism: Art in New York, Paris, and Montreal, 1945–1964* (Cambridge, Mass.: MIT Press, 1986), pp. 244–310, esp. pp. 279 ff.

Notes to Baskerville, "The Act of Signifyin(g) in Popular Music"

1. John W. Blassingame, *The Slave Community: Plantation Life in the Antebellum South* (New York: Oxford University Press, 1979), p. 20.

2. Henry Louis Gates, Jr., *The Signifyin(g) Monkey: A Theory of African-American Literary Criticism* (New York: Oxford University Press, 1988), p. 6.

3. Samuel A. Floyd, Jr., "Ring Shout!: Literary Studies, Historical Studies, and Black Music Inquiry," *Black Music Research Journal* 11 (1991), pp. 265–87; Gates, p. 6.

4. Clifford Geertz, "Thick Description: Toward an Interpretive Theory of Culture," *The Interpretation of Cultures* (New York: Basic Books, 1973).

5. George E. Marcus and Michael M. J. Fischer, *Anthropology as Cultural Critique: An Experimental Moment in the Human Sciences* (Chicago: University of Chicago Press, 1986), p. 26.

6. Bruce Tucker, editor's introduction, "Black Music after Theory," *Black Music Research Journal* 11 (1991), p. vii.

7. Gates, p. 42.

8. Gates, p. 51.

9. Gates, p. 52.

10. Gary Tomlinson, "Cultural Dialogues and Jazz: A White Historian Signifies," *Black Music Research Journal* 11 (1991), pp. 231–32.

11. In the first chapter of his acclaimed but little-known novel of the Jim Crow South, C. Eric Lincoln provides one of the clearest demonstrations and explanations of "playing the dozens" to be found in a single source. Lincoln draws attention to the implacable powerlessness of black manhood in Jim Crow society, and describes "playing the dozens" and "talking that talk" as "narcotizing the black boys who were on their way to manhood"—a linguistic quasi-bootcamp training for "the white man's style of black denigration." C. Eric Lincoln, *The Avenue, Clayton City* (New York: William Morrow, 1988), pp. 11–31. In a recent book, Gates acknowledges (signifies on?) Lincoln's contribution and his "impulse to preserve" black vernacular culture. Henry Louis Gates, *Loose Canons* (New York: Oxford University Press, 1992), pp. 143–45.

12. Cross-cultural puns are not lost on Gates. As he notes, "signification" is a specialized term in deconstructionist literary studies, which, when juxtaposed with the metaphorical relation of signifyin(g) to black literary criticism, forms a complex, open-ended figurative matrix of intercultural revision and intertextuality. See Gates, *The Signifyin(g) Monkey*, pp. 44–51.

13. Floyd, p. 271.

14. Nathan Irvin Higgins, *Black Odyssey: The Afro-American Ordeal in Slavery* (New York: Vintage Books, 1977).

15. See Melville J. Herskovits, "What Has Africa Given America?" *New Republic* 84 (1935), pp. 92–94 and *The Myth of the Negro Past* (Boston: Beacon Press, 1941).

16. C. Vann Woodward, "Clio with Soul," *Journal of American History* 56 (1969), p. 17.

17. Blassingame, p. 100.

18. Alice Walker, "Nineteen Fifty-Five," *You Can't Keep a Good Woman Down: Stories* (New York: Harcourt Brace Jovanovich, 1981), p. 8.

19. John Edward Phillips, "The African Heritage of White America," *Africanism in American Culture*, Joseph E. Holloway, ed. (Bloomington: Indiana University Press, 1990), p. 230.

20. Phillips, p. 230; in an endnote, Phillips makes reference to many Swiss yodelers touring the United States and possibly being influenced by black yodeling (p. 238).

21. Eileen Southern, *The Music of Black Americans: A History*, 2nd ed. (New York: W.W. Norton & Co., 1971), p. 82.

22. Southern, p. 85.

23. Southern, pp. 444–45.

24. It should be noted that a distinctly different type of gospel song developed in the black folk churches, during and after the Protestant City Revival Movement, called "gospel blues." Thomas A. Dorsey is considered the to be the father of gospel blues; see Southern, pp. 445–56, and Michael W. Harris, *The Rise of Gospel Blues: The Music of Thomas Andrew Dorsey in the Urban Church* (New York: Oxford University Press, 1992).

25. Charlie Gillett, *The Sound of the City: The Rise of Rock and Roll* (New York: Pantheon Books, 1983), p. x.

26. Gillett, p. x.

27. Gillett, p. x.

28. Gillett, p. x; even though black music has been accommodated by the entertainment and media industries, blacks themselves are still rare among the holders of higher, more powerful positions in the music business.

29. Larry Geller and Joel Spector, with Patricia Romanowski, *If I Can Dream: Elvis' Own Story* (New York: Simon & Schuster : 1989), pp. 115–16.

30. Elaine Dundy, *Elvis and Gladys* (New York: Macmillan, 1985), p. 13.

31. Geller and Spector, p. 116.

32. Geller and Spector, p. 154.

33. The combining of the secular world with the sacred is an Africanism that was retained by blacks in the New World. Black gospel blues combined the blues with the black spiritual and hymns. In 1959, Ray Charles released "What'd I Say?"; this became the prototype of the soul sound. According to Charlie Gillett, "The song developed into a re-creation of a revivalist meeting, with Charles declaring his love for a woman instead of God but screaming, preaching, and haranguing his congregation in an otherwise authentic manner"; see Gillett, p. 202.

34. Jackie Wilson was the most influential on Elvis' movements. During the "Million Dollar Quartet" recording session with Carl Perkins, Jerry Lee Lewis, and Johnny Cash, Elvis made continual references to Wilson's performance of "Don't Be Cruel" at a Las Vegas nightclub. Elvis would eventually adopt Wilson's manner during his performance on the "Ed Sullivan Show" in 1957, where he was filmed only from the waist up; see Dundy, p. 213.

35. Geller and Spector, p. 116.

36. James Brown and Bruce Tucker, *James Brown: The Godfather of Soul* (New York: Macmillan, 1986), pp. 165–66.

37. Brown and Tucker, p. 166.

Notes to Ebersole, "The God and Goddess of the Written Word"

1. Nick Cave, "Tupelo," in *Mondo Elvis*, ed. Lucinda Ebersole and Richard Peabody (New York: St. Martin's, 1993), p. 2.

2. Laura Kalpakian, *Graced Land* (New York: Grove Weidenfeld, 1992), p. 6.

3. Kalpakian, p. 31.

4. Janice Eidus, "Elvis, Axl and Me," in *Mondo Elvis*, p. 94.

5. Michael Wilkerson, "The Elvis Cults," in *Mondo Elvis*, p. 196.

6. Rafael Alvarez, "The Annunciation," in *Mondo Elvis*, p. 170.

7. "Amazing Graceland," editorial, *Washington Post,* January 30, 1994.

8. Judy Grahn, *The Work of a Common Woman* (Oakland, Calif.: Diana Press, 1978), p. 31.

9. Grahn, pp. 31–32.

10. Sam Staggs, *MMII: The Return of Marilyn Monroe* (New York: Donald I. Fine, 1991), p. 293.

11. Rosanne Daryl Thomas, *The Angel Carver* (New York: Random House, 1993), p. 44.

Notes to Vikan, "Graceland as *Locus Sanctus*"

1. This article is adapted from *Saint Elvis*, a book-length study in preparation.

2. Peter Brown, *The Cult of the Saints: Its Rise and Function in Latin Christianity* (Chicago: University of Chicago Press, 1982); Richard Kieckhefer and G. D. Bond, eds., *Sainthood: Its Manifestations in World Religions* (Berkeley: University of California Press, 1988); Stephen Wilson, ed., *Saints and Their Cults: Studies in Religious Sociology, Folklore, and History* (New York: Cambridge University Press, 1983).

3. "Thousands Worship Elvis and He Answers Prayers," *Globe* (January 9, 1990).

4. "Saint Elvis," *Washington Post* (August 13, 1987).

5. May Man, *Elvis, Why Won't They Leave You Alone?* (New York: New American Library, 1982).

6. Albert Harry Goldman, *Elvis* (New York: McGraw-Hill, 1981).

7. Max Weber, *Economy and Society I–III* (New York: Bedminster Press, 1968), I, 241.

8. "In a Most Unsaintly City, a Bandit Wears a Halo," *New York Times* (May 11, 1989).

Days Inn Motel, Window Decorating Contest.

9. Larry Geller and Joel Spector, with Patricia Romanowski, *If I Can Dream: Elvis' Own Story* (New York: Simon & Schuster, 1989), pp. 137–40, 187.

10. Raymond A. Moody, Jr., *Elvis After Life: Unusual Psychic Experiences Surrounding the Death of a Superstar* (Atlanta: Peachtree Publishers, 1987).

11. *Weekly World News,* (December 29, 1987).

12. Hippolyte Delehaye, "Les Origines du culte des martyrs," *Subsidia hagiographica* 30 (1933); André Grabar, *Martyrium: Recherches sur le culte des reliques et l'art*

Meditation Garden, Elvis Grave veneration.

chrétien antique, I, II (Paris: College de France, 1946); Bernhard Kötting, *Peregrinatio Religiosa: Wallfahrten in der Antike und das Pilgerwesen in der alten Kirche* (Munster: Regensburg, 1950); Pierre Maraval, *Lieux saints et pèlerinages d'orient* (Paris: Cerf, 1985); *Jerusalem Pilgrims before the Crusades*, trans. John Wilkinson (Warminster: Aris & Phillips, 1977).

13. John Wilkinson, "The Tomb of Christ: An Outline of Its Structural History," *Levant* 1 (1969): 83–97; *Jerusalem Pilgrims before the Crusades; Jerusalem Pilgrimage: 1099-1185*, trans. John Wilkinson with Joyce Hill and W. F. Ryan (London: Hakluyt Society, 1988).

Meditation Garden, votive.

14. Mary Lee Nolan and Sidney Nolan, *Christian Pilgrimage in Modern Western Europe* (Chapel Hill: University of North Carolina Press, 1989); Victor Turner and Edith Turner, *Image and Pilgrimage in Christian Culture: Anthropological Perspectives* (New York: Columbia University Press,1978).

15. Elizabeth Kay, *Chimayó Valley Traditions* (Santa Fe: Ancient City Press, 1987).

16. Peter W. L. Walker, *Holy City, Holy Places?: Christian Attitudes to Jerusalem and the Holy Land in the Fourth Century* (Oxford: Clarendon Press, 1990).

17. *Orthodox Faith* 4.11. The Fathers of the Church 37 (Washington, D.C.: Catholic University of America Press, 1958), pp. 165 ff.

18. Epistle 49:402.

19. A. Stuiber, "Eulogia," *Reallexikon für Antike und Christentum* 6 (1966): 900–28.

20. Wilkinson, *Jerusalem Pilgrims Before the Crusades*, p. 83.

21. Brown, p. 50. At the gathering marking the fifteenth anniversary of Elvis' death, Anita Massey, a middle-aged nurse from Big Spring, Texas, vowed that once her son had finished high school, she was going to move to Memphis permanently. "It's because I love Elvis and I want to be where he grew up. He has become part of what we are. We're not Elvis fans, we're Elvis friends." ("We're not Elvis Fans, We're Elvis Friends," *The Commercial Appeal*, August 16, 1992.) The group designation "Elvis Friends" is more descriptive than fan, devotee, "Presleyterian" ("The Elvis Cult Has the Makings of a Rising New Religion," *Time,* October 10, 1988) or "Elfan" (Jane Stern and Michael Stern, *Elvis World* [New York: Knopf, 1987]), since it reveals at once the relationship of the individuals to the deceased and the interrelationship among the individuals.

22. Lionel Casson, *Travel in the Ancient* World (London: Allen & Unwin, 1974), pp. 262–91, 300–29.

23. Wilkinson, *Jerusalem Pilgrims Before the Crusades*, pp. 79–89.

24. Since the notion of "sight-seeing" for its own sake, which had been part of elite culture during the Greco-Roman period, seems to have all but disappeared during the leaner, more spiritually focused Middle Ages, one would not expect anything close to the lopsided tourists-to-pilgrim ratio at Graceland to have obtained in fourth-century Jerusalem. Nowadays, Vatican City provides a closer parallel, insofar as it annually draws millions of each sort of visitor, many of whom alternatively assume both identities.

25. The second most critical Elvis holiday is January 8, his birthday, and after that comes Christmas and then Mother's Day, reflecting Elvis' deep family ties and his reverence for his mother, Gladys. And the list goes on: calendars are sold highlighting three or four days every month of special Elvis significance, including the birthday of Lisa Marie (February 1), the day Elvis was discharged from the army (March 5), Elvis' wedding anniversary (May 1), and the day Elvis was divorced (October 9).

26. The August Elvis pilgrim was poetically evoked on

site by Elvis Friend Selby Townsend on the August 14, 1987, "Nightline" segment entitled "Remembering Elvis":

Most of the women are in their thirties and forties. They tease their hair, chew gum, swear, drink Pepsi Cola, smoke cigarettes, and dress too young for their years. They come here in Chevies and Fords, some in pretty bad shape, with bumper stickers, loud mufflers, and a loan on the title. No telling how long they saved for the trip. And the men, they come with short hair slicked to perfection, rolled-up short sleeves, a pack of Luckies in their shirt pocket, and white socks on their feet. Most of them went to high school, and some even finished. And they all know what it's like to work for a livin'. As I sit here in the Hickory Log on Elvis Presley Boulevard, I'm proud to be one of those very special people. My clothes come from K-Mart, my hands are rough and ugly from too many years in the beauty shop, and my only real jewelry is my wedding band. I've got a run in my pair of panty hose, and I'm soaking wet, just like the rest, from [having been] out walking in the rain to visit the grave of Elvis Presley. We are the blue-collar workers, the fans, the believers in magic and fairytales. We're not smart enough not to fall in love with someone we never met. We're not rich enough to buy everything we want from the souvenir shops. We don't even have sense enough to come in out of the rain. But Lord, we've got something special.

Only one that feels it can understand it. We share the sweetness, the emptiness, the understanding. We're the Elvis generation—wax fruit on our kitchen table, Brand X in our cabinet, a mortgage on our home, Maybelline on our eyes, and love on our hearts that cannot be explained or rained out. He was one of us.

27. Wilkinson, *Jerusalem Pilgrims Before the Crusades*, p. 77.

28. "Words on the Wall Leave Heartfelt Passions to Elvis," Baltimore *Evening Sun* (August 13, 1987).

29. Turner and Turner. The authors also emphasize the porous boundary between pilgrimage and tourism: "a tourist is half a pilgrim . . . a pilgrim is half a tourist," p. 20.

30. *Elvis Fever*, fan club quarterly, Baltimore (Fall 1988).

31. "11th Annual Candlelight Service, August 15, 1989" (brochure, Elvis Country Fan Club, Austin, Texas).

32. While it is known that Elvis was reading, or at least looking at, pornography on the toilet when he was stricken with his drug-induced heart attack, (Charles C. Thompson II and James P. Cole, *The Death of Elvis: What Really Happened* [New York: Delacorte, 1991] p. 30 ff.), the saint-making story was soon promulgated, apparently from within Graceland, that what he had taken with him to the bathroom that morning was "a religious book on the Shroud of Turin" (Lee Cotten, *The Elvis Catalog: Memorabilia, Icons, and Collectibles Celebrating The King Of Rock 'n' Roll* [Garden

City, N.Y.: Doubleday, 1987], p. 217).

33. Early ritual contact with the sacred involved sight as an extension of touch (Brown, p. 11), since it was then believed that it was through invisible contact with the object seen that the eye is able to see.

Days Inn Motel, window.

34. M. Broshi and G. Barkay, "Excavations in the Chapel of St. Vartan in the Holy Sepulchre," *Israel Exploration Journal* 35 (1985): 125–28.

35. Kötting, pp. 398–402; Maraval, pp. 230–33; Gary Vikan, "Icons and Icon Piety in Early Byzantium," *Byzantine East, Latin West: Art Historical Studies in Honor of Kurt Weitzmann* (Princeton: Princeton University Press, 1995).

36. C. Austin Miles, "In the Garden," 1912.

37. "Perón's Missing Hands: Police Find Trail Elusive," by Shirly Christian, *New York Times* (September 6, 1987). The article suggests that the hand-stealing was a variant on the body veneration traditionally extended to Eva Perón:

The Fans' Memorial Wall, votive.

The theft of the hands seemed to fit into the pattern of the two-decade-long battle for possession of the body of one of Mr. Perón's wives, Eva. . . . After Eva Perón died of cancer in 1952 at the age of 33, her body was permanently embalmed and left on display at the headquarters of the General Federation of Labor, whose members revere her still today as someone who approaches sainthood.

38. S. R. Tucker, "Pentacostalism and Popular Culture in the South: A Study of Four Musicians," *Journal of Popular Culture* 16 (1982): 68–80.

39. "Saint Elvis," *Washington Post* (August 13, 1987); "New Fast-Growing Sect Worships Elvis Presley as a God," *Baltimore Sun* (July 26, 1988); "Elvis Used Miracle Healing Power to Cure Sick Fans," *Baltimore Sun* (December 19, 1989); "Thousands Worship Elvis and He Answers Prayers," *Boston Globe* (January 9, 1990).

The Fans' Memorial Wall, votive.